FORMAL LOGIC: ITS SCOPE AND LIMITS

FORMAL LOGIC: ITS SCOPE AND LIMITS

Second Edition

Richard Jeffrey
Professor of Philosophy
Princeton University

McGraw-Hill Book Company
New York   St. Louis   San Francisco   Auckland
Bogotá   Hamburg   Johannesburg   London   Madrid
Mexico   Montreal   New Delhi   Panama   Paris
São Paulo   Singapore   Sydney   Tokyo   Toronto

This book was set in Melior by Monotype Composition Company, Inc.
The editors were Rhona Robbin and Susan Gamer;
the designer was Robin Hessel;
the production supervisor was Leroy A. Young.
The drawings were done by Monotype Composition Company, Inc.
R. R. Donnelley & Sons Company was printer and binder.

FORMAL LOGIC: ITS SCOPE AND LIMITS

2 3 4 5 6 7 8 9 0   DODO   8 9 8 7 6 5 4 3 2 1

The initial letters at the beginnings of chapters are from Raymond A. Ballinger,
Lettering Art in Modern Use: Student Edition, Van Nostrand Reinhold Company,
New York, 1965. Copyright © 1965 by Litton Educational Publishing, Inc. Repro-
duced by permission.

"Everybody Loves My Baby" (page 90), words and music by Jack Palmer and
Spencer Williams, copyright © 1924 by MCA Music, A Division of MCA, Inc., New
York, New York. Copyright renewed. Used by permission. All rights reserved. For
the British Commonwealth of Nations (excluding Canada and Australasia) and
Europe: © 1922 Clarence Williams Music Co. (now MCA Music). Reproduced by
permission of B. Feldman & Co. Ltd. 138–140 Charing Cross Road, London WC2H
OLD. For Australia, New Zealand, Papua New Guinea: Reproduced by permission of
Allans Music Australia Pty. Ltd., Melbourne.

Library of Congress Cataloging in Publication Data

Jeffrey, Richard C
    Formal logic.

    Bibliography: p.
    Includes index
      1. Logic. I. Title.
BC71.J38 1981   160   80-23655
ISBN 0-07-032321-6

For my mother,
and in memory of my father

CONTENTS

PREFACE

This is a book for beginners, designed to familiarize them with a formal system of first-order logic in the course of a semester's study and to give them access to the discoveries defining the scope and limits of formal methods that marked the coming of age of logic in the twentieth century: Gödel's completeness and incompleteness theorems for first- and second-order logic in Chapter 7, and the Church-Turing theorem on the undecidability of first-order logic in Chapter 6.

The formal system (the tree method) is based on Raymond Smullyan's version of Evert Beth's method of semantic tableaux. (Equally justly, it could be described as a diagrammatic version of Jaakkoo Hintikka's method of model sets.) In contrast to the "natural deduction" methods whose vogue in elementary logic texts began in 1950, the tree method is thrillingly easy to understand and to use. Many agree: in 1967, this was the only introductory text to use the tree method, but it has since been joined by half a dozen others. It is this simplicity that allows students to get control of the nuts and bolts of formal logic (Chapters 1 through 5) in less than a semester, so that there is time for some of the more abstract topics in Chapters 6 and 7 and in some sections of earlier chapters (Sections 2-4, 2-5, 2-6; 3-5 through 3-8; and 4-9).

Without having set out to do so, I have largely rewritten the book for this second edition. The plan is the same as in the first edition, but many details are new, and there has been some fusion and fission of chapters, with migration of some bits and expansion of others. The main features of the result are as follows.

The (truth-functional) logic of compound statements is treated in Chapters 1 through 4. Chapter 1 presents standard material that many students will be acquainted with from high school: truth tables and the like. But Section 1-5, on probability, may add novelty and shed a revealing sidelight on deductive inference—e.g., by showing that, taken together, the premises of a valid inference should be at least as hard to believe as the conclusion.

Truth trees for "not," "and," and "or" are explained and illustrated in the first two sections of Chapter 2, followed by the necessary exercises in Section 2-3. This is deliberately short and breezy. There is nothing difficult here, and it would be a disservice to the student to suggest that there is, either by going on and on about it or by providing masses of problems to be worked.

The remainder of Chapter 2 can be omitted, or used selectively, or returned to later, at the instructor's discretion. The method introduced in the first two sections is proved adequate in Section 2-4. The proof is short and simple, but inevitably abstract. It needs to be there to show the reader that there *is* something to prove (and what, and how). My own practice is to point out the main features without trying to reproduce the proof in chalk and talk, and to recommend, but not insist, that students work through it on their own.

Section 2-5 introduces a variant of the ("reduction") tree method of the first three sections: deduction trees, i.e., direct proofs in tree form. These correspond to the "coupled trees" of the first edition, and are played down here, as there, for it is reduction trees that can be adapted almost effortlessly to yield a complete formal method for testing validity of first-order inferences, as in Chapter 5. The material on deduction trees can be omitted without loss of continuity. (My practice is to discuss and illustrate it briefly, in order to show the difference between direct and indirect proof—and to show that while they come to the same thing, the indirect proofs are simpler.)

The first half of Chapter 3 is adapted from Chapters 2 and 3 of the first edition, but the rest is new: it gives more on probability (Section 3-5), an explanation of mathematical induction (Section 3-6), and finally a proof of the compactness theorem for truth-functional logic (Section 3-8). This last section can be omitted, postponed, or passed over lightly if the instructor is so inclined: it is used here only once (i.e., at the bottom of page 175, where König's lemma is needed.

The question of adequacy of the truth-functional ("Philonian") reading of conditionals in ordinary talk was given short shrift in the first edition. Here, Chapter 4 is devoted entirely to that question. As in the first edition, I argue (at the end) for the adequacy of the truth-functional reading of indicative conditionals; but here various examples are considered, and Paul Grice's "conversational implicature" ploy is given a central role. The inevitable question about conditional probabilities ("Why aren't they probabilities of conditionals?") is asked in Section 4-9, and answered by proving David

Lewis's (1976) "trivialization result." Early in their study of probability theory, students are generally shamed out of asking the question. Lewis's argument actually answers it.

Chapter 5 begins with an extension of the tree method to identity statements (Section 5-1). Only then is quantification theory addressed. (The material in Chapters 6 and 7 of the first edition appears in Sections 5-2 through 5-6 here, with numerous new examples and problems.) The thought is that many puzzles about the interpretation of general statements turn on the fact that distinct terms can have a common referent, whereas in much of ordinary talk there are tacit suggestions to the contrary. Thus, "Everybody loves b" is intended as a generalization "$\forall x(x \neq b \to xLb)$" about everybody other than b, even though a stickler could insist that it says something stronger, i.e., "$\forall x\, xLb$." Functions are introduced in Section 5-7. Toward the end, the question of the existential import of categorical statements is treated in terms of conversational implicature (Section 5-9), and Russell's theory of descriptions is given its due.

Chapters 6 and 7 provide straightforward proofs of the main limitative results. Chapter 6 gives instruction in the programming of register machines (Joachim Lambek's "infinite abacusses"), proves that the halting problem for such programs is unsolvable, and then reduces that problem to the decision problem for first-order logic.

Only after undecidability has been proved is the completeness theorem for first-order logic addressed. Here, a point is being made: it is not undecidability but completeness whose proof requires us to become general and explicit in our treatment of the interpretation of first-order statements. The completeness proof is essentially that of Raymond Smullyan (1968)—from whose book, indeed, the whole present treatment of the tree method is adapted.

At the end of (Section 7-9), Gödel's incompleteness theorem for second-order logic is proved as a corollary of the undecidability of the fragment of first-order logic in which abacus programs are described in Section 6-5.

Many who have learned or taught from the first edition, or have commented on earlier drafts of this one, deserve thanks here, but their contributions are so numerous and varied that I despair of doing justice to them by listing names. But to George Boolos my debt is of a different order—one I would acknowledge by listing him as a second author, if he would permit it. At two points in the text I have noted particular contributions of his, but in fact he drafted parts or all of Sections 2-4, 3-8, 6-7, 7-5, 7-6, and 7-9, either to supplement the first edition in his teaching at MIT or to illustrate suggestions for this edition; and he has read and made wise suggestions about everything in the book, in one or more drafts. But in the end I have bent and shaped and rewritten everything according to my own vision, derivative and clouded though it be, so that I emerge with sole responsibility for the errors that remain. (And there is at least one falsehood in this book. That's a logical truth.)

Richard Jeffrey

FORMAL LOGIC: ITS SCOPE AND LIMITS

C H A P T E R 1

TRUTH-FUNCTIONAL INFERENCE

ogic is the science of deduction. It aims to provide systematic means for telling whether given conclusions do or do not follow from given premises, i.e., for telling whether inferences are valid or invalid. In the course of this book we shall see how that aim is partly attainable, and why it is not fully attainable.

Validity is easily defined:

> A valid inference is one whose conclusion is true in every case in which all its premises are true.

Difficulties in applying this definition arise from difficulties in canvassing all the "cases" mentioned in it. In truth-functional logic these difficulties are at a minimum. Here the cases are simply the various possibilities as to joint truth and falsity of the statements out of which the premises and conclusion are formed. Within this division of the subject the aim of logic is fully and simply attainable, for routine methods allow us to determine whether any inference is truth-functionally valid or not.

1-1   THE CONNECTIVES "NOT," "AND," "OR"

Connectives are devices that operate upon statements to produce new statements. Examples are denial, conjunction, and disjunction, corresponding to uses of the English words "not," "and," "or." These three connectives are truth-functional, i.e., the truth values (truth, falsity) of the new statements they produce are determined by the truth values of the statements upon which they operate.

Denials are most often formed by infixing the word "not" and making whatever further changes are required to restore grammatical equilibrium. In logical notation, where capital letters stand for statements, denial is indicated simply by prefixing a dash, e.g.,

A: Cows fly. $-A$: Cows do not fly.

Conjunctions are generally formed by infixing the word "and." In logical notation we form conjunctions by writing ampersands ("&") between the statements that are to be conjoined, and enclosing the result in parentheses. Thus, with

A: Alma went. B: Ben went. C: Clara went.

we would write "$(A \ \& \ B \ \& \ C)$" for either of these:

Alma went and Ben went and Clara went.

Alma, Ben, and Clara went.

The point of the parentheses is to avoid ambiguity when connectives, e.g., denial, are applied to the compound:

$-(A \ \& \ B \ \& \ C)$: Alma, Ben, and Clara did not all go.

As this example shows, the devices used for that purpose in English are more complex.

Disjunctions are commonly formed by infixing the word "or." In logical notation we use wedges to the same effect, enclosing the whole in parentheses to avoid ambiguity later:

$(A \lor B \lor C)$: Alma or Ben or Clara went.

$-(A \lor B \lor C)$: Neither Alma nor Ben nor Clara went.

Here are the rules for computing truth values of these three sorts of compounds:

RULES OF VALUATION
> Denial reverses truth value.
> Conjunctions are true if all components are true, and false if even one component is false.
> Disjunctions are true if even one component is true, and false if all components are false.

1-2   TRUTH TABLES FOR INFERENCES

We can now test inferences for validity.

Example 1: A Valid Inference

Min is home or on board.	(premise)	$(A \lor B)$
She is not home.	(premise)	$-A$
She is on board.	(conclusion)	B

There are four cases, which we list systematically as at the left of the truth table:

	A	B	$(A \lor B)$	$-A$	B
Case 1	t	t	t	f	t
Case 2	t	f	t	f	f
Case 3	f	t	t	t	t
Case 4	f	f	f	t	f

At the right of the table we list the two premises and the conclusion, and then we work out the truth values they assume in each of the four cases regarding truth values of "A" and "B." The following pattern never appears:

Premise	Premise	Conclusion
t	t	f

A case in which that pattern appeared would be a *counterexample* (to the hypothesis that the inference is valid).

Counterexamples are cases in which all premises are true but the conclusion is false. The valid inferences are those that have no counterexamples. The invalid inferences are those that have one or more counterexamples.

Example 2: An Invalid Inference

			A	B	(A ∨ B)	A	−B
Min is home or on board.	(A ∨ B)		t	t	t	t	f
She is home.	A		t	f	t	t	t
She is not on board.	−B		f	t	t	f	f
			f	f	f	f	t

Because there is a counterexample (case 1), the inference is invalid. Intuitively, the inference is invalid because nothing rules out the possibility that Min lives on board. (In the absence of indications to the contrary, we assume that "or" statements are intended as disjunctions in our sense, i.e., the "inclusive" sense, in which the case where both components are true is included among the t cases for the disjunction.)

Example 3: A Valid Inference

Min is not both home and on board.   −(A & B)
She is home.   A
_____   _____
She is not on board.   −B

A	B	−(A & B)	A	−B
t	t	f t	t	f
t	f	t f	t	t
f	t	t f	f	f
f	f	t f	f	t

If you think this inference invalid, you are probably looking under the ampersand for the truth value of "−(A & B)" instead of under the dash.

Example 4: A Valid Inference

Min is home or on board.   (A ∨ B)
Hen is home or Min is.   (C ∨ A)
Min's not home.   −A
_____   _____
Hen's home and Min's on board.   (C & B)

ABC	$(A \vee B)$	$(C \vee A)$	$-A$	$(C \& B)$
t t t	t	t	f	t
t t f	t	t	f	f
t f t	t	t	f	f
t f f	t	t	f	f
f t t	t	t	t	t
f t f	t	f	t	f
f f t	f	t	t	f
f f f	f	f	t	f

Only in case 5 are all premises true, and there the conclusion is true as well. Thus no case is a counterexample.

Example 5: A Valid Inference

Min is home or on board.	$(A \vee B)$
Hen is home or on board.	$(C \vee D)$
They are not both on board.	$-(B \& D)$
Min is home or Hen is.	$(A \vee C)$

	A	B	C	D	$A \vee B$	$C \vee D$	$-(B \& D)$	$A \vee C$
	t	t	t	t	t	t	f	t
	t	t	t	f	t	t	t	t
	t	t	f	t	t	t	f	t
	t	t	f	f	t	f	t	t
	t	f	t	t	t	t	t	t
	t	f	t	f	t	t	t	t
	t	f	f	t	t	t	t	t
	t	f	f	f	t	f	t	t
	f	t	t	t	t	t	f	t
	f	t	t	f	t	t	t	t
Case 11	f	t	f	t	t	t	f	f
Case 12	f	t	f	f	t	f	t	f
	f	f	t	t	f	t	t	t
	f	f	t	f	f	t	t	t
Case 15	f	f	f	t	f	t	t	f
Case 16	f	f	f	f	f	f	t	f

Only in cases 11, 12, 15, and 16 is the conclusion false. Then counter-examples will be found in those cases, if anywhere.

As in the column headings of this table, we shall often omit outer parentheses from conjunctions and disjunctions that stand alone rather than as components of longer statements; no ambiguity can result.

Observe that the number of cases doubles each time the number of letters increases by 1.

Number of letters: $n = 1$ 2 3 4 5 6 ... 10 ...

Number of cases: $2^n = 2$ 4 8 16 32 64 ... 1024 ...

Then even where there are only four letters, as in Example 5, we should seek to avoid needless labor by dealing with whole blocks of cases at once, if we can, in searching for counterexamples. Thus, in Example 5, the conclusion "$A \lor C$" must be false in any counterexample, and that will happen only if "A" and "C" separately are false: in cases 11, 12, 15, and 16. Then we can confine our further search for counterexamples to those four cases. There was no need to construct the full truth table.

1-3   VALID AND SATISFIABLE STATEMENTS

Sometimes conclusions are obtainable without using premises at all.

Example 6: Inference without Premises

A	$A \lor -A$
t	t
f	t

Min is home or Min is not home. $A \lor -A$

Neither case is a counterexample, for the conclusion is true in both.

Such conclusions themselves are called "valid":

> The valid statements are those true in all cases.

Truth-functionally valid statements are called "tautologies." Thus, a tautology is a statement that has an unbroken column of "t"s under its main connective when its truth table is worked out. In later chapters, where cases are not simply assignments of truth values to statement letters, we shall encounter plenty of valid statements that are not tautologies, but for the present, validity will always be truth-functional.

Example 7: One Is a Tautology, the Other Is Not

$M \vee (-M \& -H)$: Either Min is home or she and Hen are both not home.

$M \vee -(M \& H)$: Either Min is home or she and Hen are not both home.

M	H	$M \vee (-M \& -H)$		$M \vee -(M \& H)$	
t	t	t	f	t	f
t	f	t	f	t	t
f	t	f	f	t	t
f	f	t	t	t	t

The second statement is a tautology: see the solid column of "t"s under its wedge. But the first is no tautology, for it is false in case 3.

Inferences with valid conclusions are always valid, regardless of what their premises may be, for a counterexample would be a case in which the conclusion is false, and there are no such cases if the conclusion is valid.

Example 8: The Premise Is Redundant

		A	B	$A \vee -A$
Hen is home.	B	t	t	t
Min is home or not.	$A \vee -A$	t	f	t
		f	t	t
		f	f	t

Of course there is no need to work out the four-case truth table here in order to see that the inference is valid. The only point of doing it is to emphasize that "$A \vee -A$" has a definite truth value (viz., truth) in each case concerning the truth values of "A" and "B," simply because each of them is also a case concerning the truth value of "A."

If there is no case in which all premises of an inference are true, the inference counts as valid according to our definition, for it has no counterexamples.

Example 9: The Conclusion Is Redundant

			A	B	−A
Min is home.	A		t	t	f
Min is not home.	−A		t	f	f
Hen is home.	B		f	t	t
			f	f	t

A counterexample would be a row of form "t f t." There is none.

Here again there was no need to construct the truth table. The only point of doing it was to show that the straightforward truth-table test does give the right answer here, too.

The contradictory statements "A," "−A" are said to be "jointly unsatisfiable." In general:

A set of statements is said to be satisfiable if there is at least one case in which all members of the set are true. The set is said to be unsatisfiable if there is no case in which all members are true. Similarly, an individual statement is said to be satisfiable or unsatisfiable depending on whether or not there is a case in which it is true.

1-4 SOUNDNESS

Clearly, inferences whose premises form unsatisfiable sets are always valid, according to our "no counterexamples" definition of validity: from a contradiction, *anything* follows. ("If you'll believe that, you'll believe anything!") But such inferences, although unshakably valid, are equally unshakably unsound, according to this definition:

Sound = valid and with all premises true

It is the sound inferences whose conclusions are surely true; mere validity of the inference is not enough to guarantee truth of the conclusion. Nor is validity enough when coupled with mere consistency of the premises, i.e., joint truth of all of them in *some* possible case. In the definition of soundness, "truth" means truth in the *actual* case, which is what the word means in common English. And throughout this book, when we speak simply of truth (and not *truth in case such-and-such*), we mean truth in the ordinary sense. Our use of fanciful examples makes it easy to forget that there are such things as simple truth and falsity. (Does Min really live on board? There is no fact of the matter.) To illustrate soundness and un-soundness we must turn to real examples, from life.

Example 10: An Unsound, Valid Inference

		S	W	S ∨ W
Sharks are mammals.	S	t	t	t
Sharks or whales are mammals.	S ∨ W	t	f	t
		f	t	t
		f	f	f

Case 3 is the actual case.

Observe that as whales really are mammals, the conclusion is true. Neither unsoundness nor invalidity of an inference can guarantee that its conclusion will not be true.

Unsoundness is not always a defect—e.g., when we refute someone's claims by validly deducing an unsatisfiable statement from them, the inference is necessarily unsound: as the conclusion is a contradiction, it is false in every case, and therefore, as the inference is valid, there can be no case in which all premises are true. Then in particular, the actual case is one in which not all premises are true.

Example 11: *Reductio ad Absurdum*

Watson asserts that Crun and Moriarty are either both guilty or both innocent, and denies that either Crun is innocent or Moriarty is guilty. Thus he holds that $(C \& M) \lor (-C \& -M)$ and that $-(-C \lor M)$. From these two premises, Holmes deduces that Crun is both guilty and innocent $(C \& -C)$, thus proving Watson's statements inconsistent by "reduction to absurdity." (The table shows that none of the four cases is a counterexample: as usual, Holmes's deduction is impeccable.)

C	M	(C & M) ∨ (−C & −M)	−(−C ∨ M)	C & −C
t	t	t	f	f
t	f	f	t	f
f	t	f	f	f
f	f	t	f	f

Then Watson's statements include at least one falsehood, no matter which case is actual.

Notice the variety of terminology in common use. Inference is said to be a matter of *deduction* or *derivation* of a conclusion from premises. Where the inference is valid, the premises are said to *imply* the conclusion. Where the premises of a valid inference are not in doubt, we speak of *demonstration* or *proof* of the conclusion.

Less abstractly, we may speak of *argument* (sound or unsound, valid or invalid) instead of inference. The aim of argument need not be demonstration of the truth of the conclusion, for as we have seen, argument by *reductio ad absurdum* aims rather to demonstrate falsity of at least one of the premises by deducing from them an obviously false conclusion. And in other cases where the conclusion of a valid argument is hard to believe, logic is far from demanding that we swallow doubts and accept the conclusion as demonstrated. An equally logical response is to scrutinize the premises, in the expectation that the astounding inference is unsound. Reason: the "no counterexamples" definition shows that validity of an inference comes to no more than unsatisfiability of the set consisting of its premises and the denial of its conclusion. Logic forbids belief in all of these, but singles no one of them out for disbelief. Thus validity of an argument forces acceptance of the conclusion no more than it forces rejection of a premise.

1-5 PROBABILITY

The case for "following the argument wherever it may lead" is even weaker when we look at matters from a probabilistic point of view. We may think of probabilities in terms of cases as to joint truth and falsity of the statement letters that appear in an inference. With n statement letters there will be 2^n such cases, each of which has as its probability some number in the interval from 0 to 1 (inclusive), and the probabilities of all cases together must sum to 1. Then when the number of cases is finite, the following applies:

> The probability of a statement is the sum of the probabilities of the cases in which it is true.

Now the probability that the premises of an inference are all true will be the sum of the probabilities of the cases in which they are all true;

and if the inference is valid, these cases will be among those in which the conclusion is true. Therefore:

> In a valid inference, the probability that all premises are true is less than or equal to the probability that the conclusion is true.

Moral: taken collectively, the premises should be at least as hard to believe as the conclusion.

Of course, individual premises may be more probable than the conclusion. It is the conjunction of *all* the premises whose probability is limited by that of the conclusion.

Example 12: "The Lottery Paradox"

The tickets in a lottery are numbered consecutively from 1 to 1000, and just one ticket will win. Consider the inference with 1000 premises, "Ticket 1 loses," "Ticket 2 loses," . . . , "Ticket 1000 loses," and with the conjunction of all 1000 premises as its conclusion:

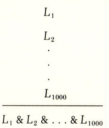

$$L_1$$

$$L_2$$

$$\vdots$$

$$L_{1000}$$

$$\overline{}$$

$$L_1 \& L_2 \& \ldots \& L_{1000}$$

If the lottery is fair, each premise is a near-certainty, having probability 99.9 percent, i.e., 999/1000, but the conclusion ("All tickets lose") is not to be believed, having probability 0. Moral: out of enough silk purses you can make a sow's ear.

The question of the meaning of probability attributions is much debated. Yesterday's orthodoxy was *frequentism* (the *relative frequency* view), according to which it is only "repeatable events" (e.g., heads on tosses of a certain coin) that have probabilities, viz., the ratios of the numbers of successes (here, heads) to the total number of trials (here, tosses). Frequentism denies significance to talk about probabilities of (truth of) statements about "unrepeatable events," e.g., the statement that the third toss of this very penny will result in a head.

On this same question, yesterday's lunatic fringe, *subjectivism* (or *personalism*), has become respectable as at least a partial account of what we mean by attributing probabilities to statements. According to the subjectivist view, probability attributions refer to the speaker (the subject) as much as to their ostensible subject matter; e.g., when I attribute probability .37 to the statement that it will rain tomorrow, I am identifying 37¢ as the price at which I would buy or sell a ticket that is worth $1 or $0 depending on whether the statement is true or false. For you, the probability (the price) might be different.

These rough characterizations of frequentism and subjectivism are good enough for present purposes: for illustrating the breadth of the gaps separating various current views, and for giving one example (subjectivism) of a view on which it makes sense to attribute probabilities to statements of all sorts. In discussing probabilities of statements here, we shall leave open the question "Where do the numbers come from?" just as earlier we left open the question "What determines the truth values of statement letters?" Just as we observed earlier that in a valid inference the conclusion must be true if all premises are, so now we observe that in a valid inference the probability that the conclusion is true is at least as great as the probability that all premises are. If determination of actual truth values is not a question for logic, still less is the determination of actual probability values—either for a person at a time, or in some objective sense. But in the extreme cases of valid statements and unsatisfiable ones, where logic suffices to determine truth value, the probability values are likewise determined: being true in all cases, valid statements must have probability 1, while unsatisfiable statements must have probability 0 because they have no t cases.

1-6 PROBLEMS

1. Does a imply b? Does b imply a? Where implication fails, identify all counterexamples.
   (a) You and I will bail or we shall sink.
   (b) You will bail and either I shall bail or we shall sink.

2. Test the validity of Watson's inference. "Crun is guilty," observed Watson, "because (a) either Holmes is right and the vile Moriarty is guilty, or he is wrong and the scurrilous Crun did the job; but (b) those scoundrels are either both guilty or both innocent; and as usual, (c) Holmes is right." (Is Watson being dense, as usual?)

3. Display the following on a common, four-case truth table. Use "M" and "C" for "Moriarty is guilty" and "Crun is guilty."
   (a) Either Moriarty and Crun are both guilty or Crun is innocent.
   (b) Either Crun is guilty or both he and Moriarty are.

(c) Either Moriarty is guilty or both he and Crun are innocent.
(d) Either Moriarty is guilty or Crun is innocent or both are guilty.
(e) They are not both guilty, and at least one is innocent.
(f) Either both are guilty or Moriarty is but Crun is not.
(g) Either they are not both guilty or they are not both innocent.

Which are tautologies? Among the rest, which imply which others? Which imply that Moriarty is guilty? Which imply that Crun is guilty? The seven statements a to g are not jointly satisfiable, but certain six-membered subsets are. Which? Which of the seven are individually satisfiable?

4. True or false?
   (a) If a statement is not valid, its denial must be.
   (b) If a statement is not satisfiable, its denial is valid.
   (c) If a statement fails to imply an other, it must imply the denial of that other.
   (d) A statement that implies an other cannot imply the denial of that other.
   (e) If a set of statements is satisfiable, so is each statement in the set.
   (f) If each statement in a set is satisfiable, so is the set.
   (g) You cannot make a valid inference invalid by adding more premises.
   (h) You cannot make an invalid inference valid by removing premises.

5. Given that the probabilities of the four cases are as shown below, work out the probabilities of statements a to g in problem 3 above:

M	C	Proba-bility
t	t	.4
t	f	.3
f	t	.2
f	f	.1

6. Suppose that we have much less information about probability than is given in problem 5: suppose that we only know that none of the four cases has probability 0. Which of a to g can still be identified as definitely more probable than which others?

7. A coin is tossed three times. "A," "B," and "C" mean that it lands head up on the first, second, and third tosses, respectively. Suppose that the eight cases are equiprobable. Translate the following statements into or out of logical notation, and find the probability of each statement. Which imply which others?
   (a) All tosses are heads.
   (b) $-A \lor -B \lor -C$
   (c) $-A \ \& -B \ \& -C$
   (d) All tosses have the same outcome.
   (e) $(A \ \& \ B) \lor (-A \ \& -B)$
   (f) There is at least one head.
   (g) There is at most one head.
   (h) There are an odd number of heads.

8. What does someone take to be the probability that the weather will be the same on both days (i.e., rain on both or on neither) who takes the statement "It will rain tomorrow *and* the next day" to have the same probability as the statement "It will rain tomorrow *or* the next day"? Explain, briefly.

9. *Knights and Knaves.* Knaves always lie, knights always tell the truth, and in Transylvania, where everybody is one or the other (but you can't tell which by looking) you encounter two people, one of whom tells you, "He's a knight or I'm a knave." What are they?*

10. *Cretans.*† "One of themselves, even a prophet of their own, said: The Cretans are always liars, evil beasts, slow bellies." So Paul says, adding, "This witness is true." Is *that* true?

1-7 SENTENCES AND STATEMENTS

Strictly speaking, statements are not sentences. Rather, we use sentences to *make* statements, as when I utter the sentence "Father knew Lloyd George" in order to tell my wife (falsely, in fact) that M. M. Jeffrey knew the prime minister. But not every occasion on which a declarative sentence is spoken or written or tapped out in Morse code is an occasion on which a statement is thereby made; the sentence might have been uttered as part of a song, or written to practice calligraphy, or tapped out to test the circuit. Nor are sentences the only vehicles for statement making; in suitable circumstances a shrug or a nod or a silence will do the job.

It often happens that the same declarative sentence can be used to make one statement or another, depending on who utters it, when and where it is uttered, to whom it is addressed, and with what accompanying gestures or conversational context: "I saw you chatting with him here yesterday" is a case in point. The conversational context might determine the referent of "him," e.g., perhaps the sentence is addressed to someone who has just said, "I haven't seen Henry Crun in years." But the nonconversational context (e.g., place and time of utterance) may be equally important in determining what statement, if any, the speaker or writer or telegrapher, etc., makes by a particular act of speaking or writing or telegraphing, etc.

---

* Thanks to Raymond Smullyan, *What Is the Name of This Book?* Prentice-Hall, Englewood Cliffs, N.J., 1978.
† Thanks to Paul of Tarsus, Epistle to Titus, I, 12.

Difficulties about context dependence are at a minimum in scientific and mathematical discourse. If we were concerned only with sentences like "Whales are mammals" and "There are infinitely many prime numbers," we could ignore the fact that it is people, not sentences, that make statements—for (nearly enough) anyone, anywhere, any time, who utters such a sentence thereby makes the same statement that anyone else would, anywhere, any time, etc., by uttering that sentence. But except in such carefully controlled circumstances, context dependency is as pervasive as the air we breathe, and as unobtrusive. It does not cross our minds that two people might be contradicting each other when one says, "I went to Granchester yesterday," and the other replies, "I did not"; nor are we tempted to symbolize the second statement by "−A" once we have used "A" for the first. We cope with context dependency as easily and as unconsciously as we breathe, in ordinary circumstances.

But when in logic we formulate general truths about validity, unsatisfiability, etc., it is a great help to be able to ignore the distinction between sentence and statement, as we can, quite safely, if we can depend upon all the sentences we meet to be context-independent. To arrange that, we imagine that English has been replaced by a well-behaved artificial language called "Logic" with a capital "L." (Less fancifully: we use logical notation in place of English.) In Logic we eliminate context dependency by fixing truth values of statement letters so as to leave them unaffected by subsequent contexts of use. Thus, in the banal exchange about Granchester, we interpret "A" as a context-independent sentence which, uttered by anyone, any time, produces a statement that can be depended upon to have the same truth value as the statement that the first speaker made by saying "I went to Granchester yesterday."

The grammatical rules of this artificial language are quite simply stated, being strikingly uniform in contrast to the corresponding rules of English grammar. The first of them provides an initial stock of sentences, and the rest give ways of forming new sentences out of old. As there will be no context dependency once the initial stock of sentences has been interpreted, we cheerfully ignore the distinction between sentence and statement.

RULES OF FORMATION
  0. Capital letters, with or without numerical subscripts, count as
     statements.
  Further statements are formed by the following operations.
  1. **Denial:** prefix a dash to a statement.
  2. **Conjunction:** write ampersands between adjacent members of a
     finite sequence of two or more statements, and enclose the
     result in parentheses.
  3. **Disjunction:** write wedges between adjacent members of a finite
     sequence of two or more statements, and enclose the result in
     parentheses.

Until Chapter 4, nothing counts as a statement (= sentence) of Logic
unless it either is a statement letter or can be obtained from statement letters by a finite number of uses of operations 1, 2, and 3.

The rules of valuation given in Section 1-1 for determining truth
values of compound statements are keyed to these rules of formation.
A denial is true/false if formed from a false/true statement. A conjunction is true/false if all/some of the statements from which it was
formed are true/false. A disjunction is true/false if some/all of the
statements from which it was formed are true/false. But for statement
letters we give no general rules of valuation. Their truth values are
assigned ad hoc as in the following familiar sort of example.

Example 13: Interpretation of Oral Argument

Neddy:	They're not both on board, Jim!	$-(A \& B)$
Jim:	Ah, but *she* is.	A
Neddy:	Then he isn't, Jim!	$-B$

Clearly, just two people are under discussion, of different sexes. In
logical notation the second premise, "A," is interpreted as having the
same truth value as Jim's statement, whichever that may be, and
similarly in the conclusion, the statement letter "B" is assigned a
truth value (t or f, as may be) opposite to that of Neddy's final statement. Once those assignments have been made, it is clear that either
"$-(A \& B)$" or "$-(B \& A)$" will do as a context-independent vehicle
for making a statement having the same truth value as Neddy's
opening remark.

For the most part, logical notation is parasitic upon ordinary talk in such ways as we have just illustrated. Truth values of statement letters are fixed (until further notice) in relation to the truth values of certain actual statements. But we need not know those statements' truth values at the time we make those stipulations, or, indeed, ever. Similarly the khan's subjects can promise him his weight in gold without being able to put a number to it either when they make the promise or when they keep it by loading gold onto one side of a balance until the khan, on the other, rises just clear of the ground.

CHAPTER 2

TRUTH TREES

A test for validity is an exhaustive search for counterexamples, with success of the search showing invalidity of the inference under test, and failure showing validity. The truth-table test of Chapter 1 is straightforward but needlessly laborious when statement letters are numerous, for the number of cases to be searched doubles with each additional letter (so that, e.g., with 10 letters there are over 1000 cases). The truth-tree test that will now be presented is equally straightforward but saves labor by searching whole blocks of cases at once.

Examples 1 and 2

To begin, we illustrate the tree test by applying it simultaneously to Examples 1 and 2 of Chapter 1: see Figure 2-1.

Figure 2-1   Tree test applied to Examples 1 and 2 of Chapter 1.

Example 1				Example 2			
$A \vee B$	1	$\sqrt{A \vee B}$	(prem)	$A \vee B$	1	$\sqrt{A \vee B}$	(prem)
$-A$	2	$-A$	(prem)	A	2	A	(prem)
B	3	$-B$	(−concl)	B	3	$-B$	(−concl)
	4	$A \quad B$	(from 1)		4	$A \quad B$	(from 1)
		$\times \quad \times$				$\times$	
Valid: There are no counter-examples.				Invalid: The left-hand path describes a counterexample.			

In each case we begin the tree by listing the premises and the *denial* of the conclusion: lines 1 to 3. Those statements will be true in exactly the cases that are counterexamples, for counterexamples are cases in which the premises are all true and the conclusion *false*. Then the two beginnings are as shown in Figure 2-2*a*. In each tree, lines 2 and 3 are simply statement letters or denials of such. There is nothing further to be done with them, for it is clear in which cases they are true. But in each tree, line 1 is a disjunction, and requires analysis: "*A* ∨ *B*" is true in all cases in which "*A*" is true and in all cases in which "*B*" is true, and is true in no other cases. We indicate all that by writing "*A*" and "*B*" at the ends of two branches at the bottom of the tree (Figure 2-2*b*). At the same time we check (√) the statement "*A* ∨ *B*" to show that all its t cases have been taken into account. *Checking a line is equivalent to crossing it out or erasing it.* Finally we write "×" at the bottom of each path in which a statement occupies one line and its denial occupies another (Figure 2-2*c*). Such paths are said to be "closed." *There are no cases in which all lines of a closed path are true statements.* Figure 2-2*c* shows the finished trees for the two inferences. The annotations of the two trees shown in Figure 2-1 (the numbers at the left and the parenthetical remarks at the right) are not parts of the trees themselves, but are added to facilitate discussion by showing the source of each line. Later in this chapter (Section 2-4) we shall see that the method is *correct* in the sense that *the valid inferences are those in whose finished trees all paths are closed.* ("Finished" means that no more rules apply.)

Figure 2-2   Growth of the two trees.

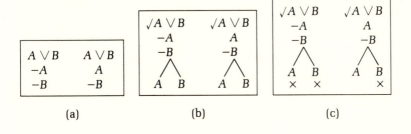

(a)   (b)   (c)

2-1 RULES OF INFERENCE

The treatment of disjunction in the foregoing examples can be summarized diagrammatically as follows:

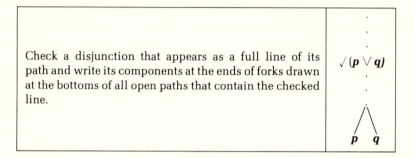

In the diagram, "*p*" and "*q*" stand for the two components of a disjunction that appears as a full line of the path represented by the dots, e.g., in our two examples "*p*" stands for "*A*" and "*q*" for "*B*," so that "*p* ∨ *q*" stands for "*A* ∨ *B*." The outer parentheses are exhibited in the formal statement of the rule even though we often omit them in practice. The diagram summarizes the instructions given in English at the left. Observe that we are *not* entitled to check disjunctions where they stand as components of longer statements, as, e.g., in "−(*A* ∨ *B*)" or in "(*A* ∨ *B*) & *C*." But we *are* entitled to check "−(*A* & *B*) ∨ *C*" where it stands as a full line of a path, as illustrated schematically in Figure 2-3. There, "*p*" and "*q*" stand for "−(*A* & *B*)" and "*C*" in the rule for *p* ∨ *q*, above, and the check mark applies to the disjunction "−(*A* & *B*) ∨ *C*" as a whole. It is to make that quite clear that the outer parentheses were included: "(−(*A* & *B*) ∨ *C*)."

Figure 2-3

The rule for denied conjunctions is much like that for disjunctions:

Check a denied conjunction that stands as a full line of its path and write denials of its components at the ends of forks drawn at the bottoms of all open paths that contain the checked line.	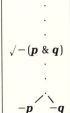

Rationale: a conjunction is false (its denial is true) when either component is false, and only then.

Example 3: A Valid Inference

Min is not both home and
　on board.　　　　$-(A \& B)$　1　$\checkmark -(A \& B)$　(prem)
She is home.　　　　　A　　2　　　A　　(prem)

She is not on board.　　$-B$　　3　　$--B$　　(−concl)

4　$-A$　$-B$　(from 1)
　　$\times$　$\times$

Observe that the right-hand path is closed because it contains a statement ("$-B$") together with its denial ("$--B$"). No matter that the statement "$-B$" is not a single letter!

Example 4: A Valid Inference

Min is home or on board.　$A \vee B$　1　$\checkmark A \vee B$　(prem)
Hen is home or Min is.　$C \vee A$　2　$\checkmark C \vee A$　(prem)
Min's not home.　　　$-A$　　3　　$-A$　　(prem)

Hen's home and Min's　　$C \& B$　4　$\checkmark -(C \& B)$　(−concl)
　on board

5　A　　B　(from 1)
　$\times$

6　　C　A　(from 2)
　　　　$\times$

7　$-C$　$-B$　(from 4)
　$\times$　$\times$

As all paths are closed, the inference is valid.

Example 5: A Valid Inference

This example requires the rules already introduced together with a new rule, for denied disjunction:

Check a denied disjunction where it appears as a full line of its path and write denials of its components in a column at the bottom of each open path that contains the checked line.	$\cdot$ $\cdot$ $\cdot$ $\sqrt{-(p \vee q)}$ $\cdot$ $\cdot$ $\cdot$ $-p$ $-q$

Rationale. A disjunction is false (its denial is true) in exactly the cases in which *both* components are false, i.e., the cases in which their denials are both true.

Min is home or on board.	$A \vee B$	1	$\sqrt{A \vee B}$	(prem)
Hen is home or on board.	$C \vee D$	2	$\sqrt{C \vee D}$	(prem)
They are not both on board.	$-(B \& D)$	3	$\sqrt{-(B \& D)}$	(prem)
Min is home or Hen is.	$A \vee C$	4	$\sqrt{-(A \vee C)}$	(−concl)
		5	$-A$	(from
		6	$-C$	4)
		7	$A \qquad B$	(from 1)
			$\times$	
		8	$C \qquad D$	(from 2)
			$\times$	
		9	$-B \qquad -D$	(from 3)
			$\times \qquad \times$	

The rule for conjunctions is obvious:

Check a conjunction where it appears as a full line of its path and write its components in a column at the bottom of each open path that contains the checked line.	$\cdot$ $\cdot$ $\sqrt{(p \& q)}$ $\cdot$ $\cdot$ p q

Example 6: A Valid Inference

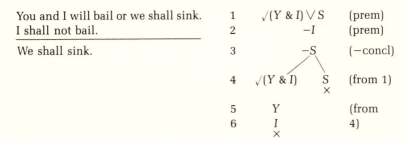

You and I will bail or we shall sink.	1	$\checkmark(Y \& I) \vee S$	(prem)
I shall not bail.	2	$-I$	(prem)
We shall sink.	3	$-S$	(−concl)
	4	$\checkmark(Y \& I) \quad S$	(from 1)
	5	Y	(from
	6	I	4)

The need for one more rule is illustrated by the following example.

Example 7: Double Denial

Min is home.	1	A	(prem)
Min is not not home.	2	$- - -A$	(−concl)
	3	$-A$	(from 2)

The inference is valid, for the sole path is closed.

The rule that takes us from line 2 to line 3 has a thrillingly simple statement:

Erase double dashes.

Rationale. As denial reverses truth values, double denial brings them back to what they were originally. But to put denial on a footing with the other connectives, we view the simple statement "Erase double dashes" as shorthand for the long-winded rule at the left below, diagrammed at the right:

If a statement beginning "− −" appears as a full line of its path, check it and write what follows the "− −" at the bottom of each open path that contains the checked statement.	$\checkmark - -p$
	p

	Denial	Conjunction	Disjunction

	Denial	Conjunction	Disjunction
Undenied	$-p$ p ――― $\times$ 0	$\sqrt{(p \ \& \ q \ \& \ r)}$ ―――――― p q r 2	$\sqrt{(p \lor q \lor r)}$ ―――――― $p \mid q \mid r$ 4
Denied	$\sqrt{--p}$ ――― p 1	$\sqrt{-(p \ \& \ q \ \& \ r)}$ ―――――― $-p \mid -q \mid -r$ 3	$\sqrt{-(p \lor q \lor r)}$ ―――――― $-p$ $-q$ $-r$ 5

Figure 2-4 Summary of tree rules.

2-2 THE TREE TEST

In a new but obvious notation, we can summarize the tree rules as in Figure 2-4. For definiteness, the rules for conjunction and disjunction show the three-component cases. The other cases are similar. In order to put denial as much as possible on a footing with the other connectives, we have treated "write '×' at the bottom of closed paths" as one of two rules for denial: the two-premise rule 0.

To test an inference for validity, write its premises and the denial of its conclusion in a column, and apply the rules to unchecked lines of open paths (checking lines to which rules 1 to 5 are being applied) until the tree is *finished*, i.e., until the only unchecked lines in open paths are statement letters and denials of statement letters, to which none of the rules apply. If all paths in the finished tree are closed (i.e., have "×" at the bottom), then the original inference was valid. But if there is even one open path in the finished tree, the inference is invalid, and each open path determines one or more counterexamples.

Example 8: Reading Counterexamples off the Finished Tree

Here the tree for an invalid inference is more or less bushy depending on which premise is checked first.

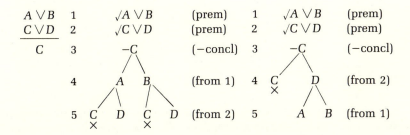

Each open path in each of these finished trees determines a class of counterexamples. For example, the left-hand open path in each tree, in which "*A*," "*−C*," and "*D*" appear as full lines but neither "*B*" nor "*−B*" appears as a full line, determines as counterexamples all cases in which "*A*," "*C*," and "*D*" are t, f, and t, respectively, regardless of the truth value of "*B*" in such cases (Figure 2-5*a*). Similarly, since "*B*," "*−C*," and "*D*" appear as full lines of the right-hand open path, but neither "*A*" nor "*−A*" does, that path determines the class of counterexamples indicated in Figure 2-5*b*. Each path determines two counterexamples, but as the ttft case for "*ABCD*" belongs to both pairs, there are three distinct counterexamples overall: ttft, tfft, ftft.

A set of statements is satisfiable when there is at least one case in which all statements in the set are true; and as we shall see (adequacy theorem), it is exactly then that there will be at least one open path through the finished tree.

This is the tree test for satisfiability of finite sets of statements:

> Start a tree with the members of the set in a column. The set is satisfiable if and only if there is an open path through the finished tree.

Figure 2-5 Counterexamples determined by open paths.

A	B	C	D
t		f	t

(a) Left

A	B	C	D
	t	f	t

(b) Right

Example 9: Satisfiability

The tree below shows that the set consisting of "*A*" and "−(*A* & *B*)" is satisfiable, for the tree is finished, and the right-hand path is open (and shows that the tf case for "*AB*" is one in which both members of the set are true):

The tree test for validity also applies to individual statements, i.e., to "inferences" without premises. The statement is a tautology if and only if the zero-premise inference to that statement as conclusion is valid.

Example 10: "(*A* & *B*) ∨ −*A* ∨ −*B*" Is a Tautology

As there are no premises, we start the tree with the denial of the conclusion (i.e., with the denial of the statement that is being tested for validity). As both paths are closed, the original (undenied) statement is shown to be a tautology:

```
1       √−((A & B) ∨ −A ∨ −B)     (−concl)
2            √−(A & B)            (from
3             − −A               line
4             − −B               1)
                /  \
5          −A        −B          (from 2)
           ×          ×
```

Then this is the tree test for validity:

> To test a statement for validity, start a tree with its *denial*. The (undenied) statement is valid if and only if all paths are closed in the finished tree.

Example 11: A Common Misconception

It may seem plausible that we can test a statement for validity by starting a tree with that statement itself (*not* its denial), concluding that the statement is a tautology if and only if every path is *open* in the finished tree. But this test is unreliable; e.g., it classifies "*A*" as a tautology and fails to classify "*A* ∨ −*A* ∨ (*A* & −*A*)" as a tautology.

2-3 PROBLEMS

Use the tree method throughout.

1. Identify all counterexamples to each of these inferences.

(a) $\dfrac{-(A \vee B)}{-A \vee -B}$ (b) $\dfrac{-A \vee -B}{-(A \vee B)}$ (c) $\dfrac{-(A \& B)}{-A \& -B}$ (d) $\dfrac{-A \& -B}{-(A \& B)}$

2. Test validity of these inferences, keeping trees as small as possible.

(a) $-A \vee B$

$-B \vee C$

$\dfrac{-C \vee D}{-A \vee D}$

(b) $\dfrac{-A \& (B \vee C)}{(-A \& B) \vee C}$

(c) $\dfrac{(-A \& B) \vee C}{-A \& (B \vee C)}$

(d) $\dfrac{A}{A}$

3. Each of the following finished trees arises in testing some inference for validity. In each case, identify the inference and annotate the tree. Where the inference is invalid, say how many (different) counterexamples there are.

(a) A

   $-A$

   $-B$

   $\times$

(b) $\sqrt{A \& -A}$

   $-B$

   A

   $-A$

   $\times$

(c) A

   $\sqrt{-(B \vee -B)}$

   $-B$

   $--B$

   $\times$

(d) $\sqrt{A \vee C \vee E}$

   $\sqrt{-(B \vee D)}$

   $-B$

   $-D$

   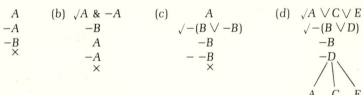

   A   C   E

4. Test the validity of this argument. "Crun is guilty, for (a) either Holmes is right and Moriarty is guilty or he is wrong and Crun is; but (b) either both are guilty or neither is; and (c) Holmes is right."

5. Does a imply b? Does b imply a?
   (a) You and I will bail or we shall sink.
   (b) You will bail and either I shall bail or we shall sink.

6. Test each of these statements for validity.
   (a) Moriarty is guilty or Crun is innocent or both are guilty.
   (b) They are not both guilty and not both innocent.

7. Find all cases in which the two statements in problem 6 are both true (together!). Then find all cases in which they are both false.

8. Is this argument sound? "Sharks or whales are mammals. Whales are mammals or fish. Thus, sharks or whales are fish."

2-4 ADEQUACY OF THE TREE TEST

The tree test can be represented as a program (Figure 2-6) applicable to an initial list of statements, viz., either the members of a set to be tested for satisfiability, or the premises together with the denial of the conclusion of an inference to be tested for validity.

The question about *length* in the third box down refers to the number of occurrences in the statement of symbols

$$(\ ) \quad - \quad \& \quad \lor \quad A \quad B \quad C \quad \ldots$$

Thus statements of length 1 and 2 are the statement letters and their denials, and statements to which rules of inference are applicable are those of length 3 or more, e.g.,

$$- -A \qquad - - -A \qquad (A \ \& \ B) \qquad -(A \ \& \ B) \qquad (A \lor B \lor C)$$

which have lengths 3, 4, 5, 6, and 7, respectively.

Figure 2-6 Tree test represented as a program.

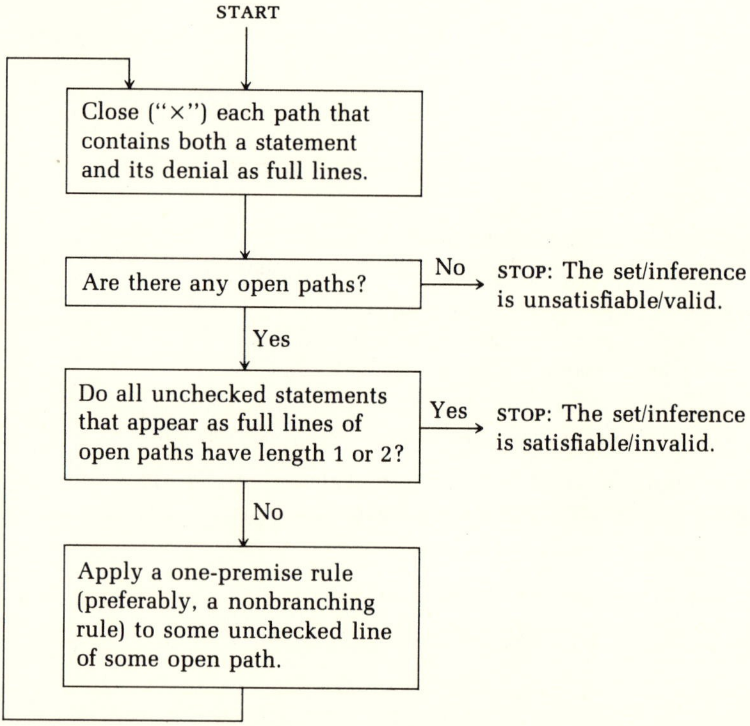

The adequacy claim for the tree test has three parts: decidability, validity correctness, and invalidity correctness. *Decidability* says that if the initial list is finite, the program always terminates, i.e., one of the two STOP arrows will be reached after some finite number of trips around the loop. (The exact number of trips will depend on the composition of the initial list.) *Validity correctness* says that the upper STOP arrow is correctly annotated, and *invalidity correctness* says the same thing about the lower STOP arrow. Thus, overall, *correctness* says that if the program does terminate, its classification of the inference (or of the set) as valid or invalid (or as unsatisfiable or satisfiable) is reliable. We now prove the three parts of the adequacy theorem in turn.

Decidability: If the initial list is finite, the tree test will terminate after some finite number of steps.

In terms of the program, a step can be identified as a passage through the bottom box: an application of a rule of inference to a line of the tree. The proof turns on the fact that when a one-premise rule is applied (checking a line and adding one or more new lines at the bottoms of open paths), *each new line is shorter than the checked line.*

Proof of decidability. Define a tree's *census* as an infinite sequence $n_1, n_2, \ldots$, where n_i is the number of unchecked lines of length i in the tree. If the tree has only finitely many lines, only a finite number of the n's are positive, and in each passage through the bottom box, checking a line and adding new lines to the tree, the census gets *smaller* in this sense: at the rightmost position where they differ (as they will), the new census has a smaller entry than the old. Now with "smaller census" so defined, every sequence of smaller and smaller censuses must come to an end after some finite number of steps, at which point we reach a STOP arrow. This completes the proof of decidability.

The proofs of the two sorts of correctness depend on the fact that the one-premise rules (1 to 5) were designed as follows:

The premise is true in exactly those valuations in which all lines in at least one list of conclusions are true (*"adequacy of the one-premise rules of inference"*).

(The rules for conjunctions and denied disjunctions each have single lists of conclusions. So does the rule for double denial, except that there the list has only one entry. But the rules for disjunctions and denied conjunctions have multiple lists of conclusions, with each list having just one entry.)

Correct annotation of the upper STOP arrow comes to this: *if there is no open path through a finished tree, the set of statements in the initial list is unsatisfiable.* Or we can put the same matter the other way around, as follows:

Validity correctness: If the initial list is satisfiable, there will be an open path through any tree that can be obtained from that list by applying rules of inference.

(These trees need not be finished, e.g., the initial list itself counts as such a tree.)

Proof of validity correctness. Suppose that in some valuation V of statement letters each full line of the initial list is true. Then the initial list must be open, for if it contained both a statement and its denial as full lines, one of those lines would be false in V. Now to prove validity correctness we need only prove that the property of *containing a full path in which all lines are true in V* is preserved when a tree having this property is extended by means of a rule of inference. Suppose then that (a) in a certain path P through an unfinished tree, all full lines are true, and that (b) we extend that tree by applying a rule of inference to one of its full lines (call it "L"). Now there are two possibilities, depending on whether or not L is in P.

If L is in P, then by (a) , L is true in V, so that by adequacy of the rule by which we extend the tree in (b), all lines in at least one list of conclusions that was then added to P will be true in V. Then P together with that list of conclusions makes up a path through the extended tree in which all full lines are true in V. Then if L is in P, the property of *containing a full path in which all lines are true in V* is preserved when the tree is extended by means of a rule of inference.

If L is not in P, then in applying a rule to L as in (b), we add nothing to P. Then here, P itself is a full path through the extended tree in which all lines are true in V.

Thus in both possibilities regarding L (i.e., on or off P) there is a full path through the extended tree in which all lines are true in V.

There must then be such a path (viz., an *open* path) through the finished tree, and the proof of validity correctness is complete.

Invalidity correctness: If there is an open path through a finished tree, the initial list is satisfiable.

Proof. Suppose that a finished tree contains an open path *P*. As the tree is finished, any line *L* of *P* having length 3 or more has been checked, and thus some list of conclusions obtained by applying a rule of inference to *L* is part of *P*. Now consider the valuation (call it "*V*") in which *statements of length 1 are true or false depending on whether or not they appear as full lines of V*. We want to show that all lines of *P* are true in V.

Notice that we defined V so as to ensure that in it, all lines of *P* that have length 1 or 2 are true.

Can any lines of *P* be false in V? If is, let *F* be a *shortest* such line; any line of *P* shorter than *F* is true in V. As the length of *F* is at least 3, one of the rules of inference applies to it. As the tree is finished, some list of conclusions obtained by applying that rule to *F* is part of *P*. But *each line of each list of conclusions is shorter than the premise F*. Therefore each line of that list must be true in V. But by the adequacy of the rule we applied to *F* to get that list, truth in V of all lines of the list implies truth in V of the premise *F* from which they came. Then our assumption that *F* is false is refuted, and invalidity correctness is proved.

2-5 DEDUCTION TREES

The trees we have been considering might aptly be called *refutation trees* or *reduction trees*: they prove validity of an inference by refuting the hypothesis that the premises together with the denial of the conclusion form a satisfiable set, and the refutation takes the form of an argument by *reductio ad absurdum*. Thus they provide what is sometimes called an "indirect proof" of the conclusion *from* the premises. In contrast, a *direct proof* would start with the premises and end with the conclusion. The deduction trees that will now be described provide such direct proofs.

Deduction trees start with the premises and end with the conclusion in each open path—if the inference is valid and the deduction has been successfully carried out. We use the familiar rules of inference together with their inverses, e.g., we use not only the familiar "analytical" rule for disjunctions, but also its two "synthetic" inverses (Figure 2-7).

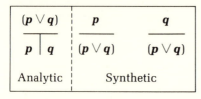

Figure 2-7
Rules for disjunction.

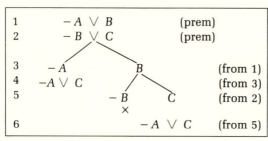

Figure 2-8
A deduction tree.

Figure 2-8 is a deduction tree for the valid inference from the premises in lines 1 and 2 to the conclusion that ends both open paths (lines 4 and 6). The new, synthetic rules are used to get "$-A \lor C$" from "$-A$" (the move from line 3 to line 4) and from "C" (from 5 to 6). Observe that the new synthetic rules are *correct* in the sense that if the premise is true in some valuation, the conclusion is also true in that valuation.

The rule that tells us to close ("×") any path that contains both a statement and its denial might be formulated as in Figure 2-9—i.e., as a rule entitling us to write any statement we please (**q**) at the bottom of a path that contains both a statement and its denial as full lines. We would then rewrite the deduction tree shown in Figure 2-8 by deleting the "×" below "$-B$" in line 5 and replacing it by the conclusion, "$-A \lor C$." So revised, a finished deduction tree for a valid inference would have the conclusion in *every* path, as in Figure 2-10, where the three paths are shown as running together at the bottom. The same deduction is shown in "tableau" form in Figure 2-11, where the line separating premises from conclusion of the inference is thought of as having been expanded (uncollapsed) into the box at the center of the tableau. In deduction tableaux, as in deduction trees, we omit the check marks ("√") that recorded applications of analytical rules in reduction trees.

The analytical rule for conjunction that we used in reduction trees made it obligatory to write *all* components in a column at the bottom of every open path containing the checked conjunction, as in

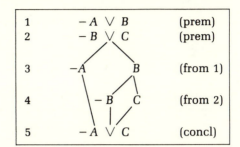

1	$-A \lor B$	(prem)
2	$-B \lor C$	(prem)
3	$-A \qquad B$	(from 1)
4	$-B \quad C$	(from 2)
5	$-A \lor C$	(concl)

Figure 2-9   Rule for denial.   Figure 2-10   Deduction tree, revised.

the reduction tree shown in Figure 2-12 for the inference from "$A \& B$" to "A." We could have formulated the rule permissively, as in Figure 2-13, thus allowing the last line, "B," to be omitted from the reduction tree. These permissive versions of the analytical rule allow us to write either component at the bottom of any path that contains the conjunction, perhaps writing different components at the bottoms of different paths and perhaps writing both components at the bottom of some path (by applying the two analytical rules in sequence). One of the permissive rules is used in the following tableau for the valid inference from "$A \& B$" to "$A \lor B$":

$$\frac{A \& B}{\dfrac{A}{A \lor B}}$$

Figure 2-11   Deduction of Figure 2-10 in tableau form.

Figure 2-12

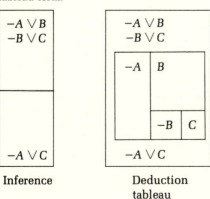

| $-A \lor B$ |
| $-B \lor C$ |
| |
| $-A \lor C$ |

Inference

$-A \lor B$	
$-B \lor C$	
$-A$	B
	$-B$ | C
$-A \lor C$	

Deduction
tableau

| $A \& B$ |
| $-A$ |
| A |
| B |
| × |

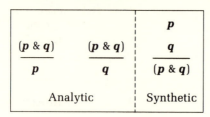

Figure 2-13   Rules for conjunction.

Of course, the rules for *denied* conjunctions and disjunctions are like those for undenied disjunctions and conjunctions, respectively (see Figure 2-14).

In moving from premises to conclusions, analytical rules take us from compound statements to their parts (or to denials of their parts), while in synthetic rules, movement is in the opposite direction. Then it is clear which is synthetic and which analytic in the pair consisting of the two rules for denied denials in Figure 2-15. But what about the rule for undenied denial, whereby we may close a path that contains both a statement and its denial as full lines, or the rule by which we have replaced that, whereby we may write any statement we please at the bottom of such a path? Somewhat arbitrarily, we shall call this new rule "analytic," and shall call "synthetic" its inverse, i.e., the new rule called "XM," shown in Figure 2-16. (Surely XM is synthetic: it doesn't take statements apart, but builds them— out of nothing!) The need for the new rule of XM is quite evident when we try to construct a deduction tree or tableau to show that a statement (e.g., "$A \lor -A$") is a tautology, for there the inference has no premises. The new rule is also needed in certain deductions from premises, e.g., in deducing "$(A \And B) \lor (A \And -B)$" from the premise "$A$" as in Figure 2-17.

"XM" stands for "excluded middle," i.e., the rule according to which there is no middle ground between truth of p and truth of $-p$: no third possibility.

Figure 2-14   (a) Rules for denied conjunctions. (b) Rules for denied disjunctions.

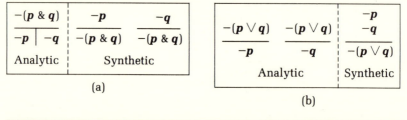

(a)

(b)

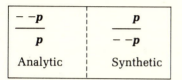

$--p$	p
p	$--p$
Analytic	Synthetic

Figure 2-15   Rules for denied denial.

p $-p$	"XM"
q	p | $-p$
Analytic	Synthetic

Figure 2-16   Rules for denial.

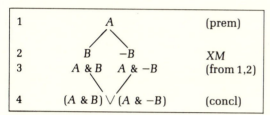

1	A	(prem)
2	$B \qquad -B$	XM
3	$A \,\&\, B \quad A \,\&\, -B$	(from 1,2)
4	$(A \,\&\, B) \vee (A \,\&\, -B)$	(concl)

Figure 2-17

We have seen that the reduction-tree test adequately achieves what we described at the beginning as the aim of logic: "to provide systematic means for telling whether given conclusions do or do not follow from given premises." Deduction trees adequately achieve the more modest aim of providing deductions of conclusions from premises if ("completeness") and only if ("correctness") the inference from those premises to that conclusion is valid.

> **Correctness:** Any statement appearing as a full line of every path through a deduction tree is implied by the initial list.
>
> **Completeness:** For any valid inference there is a deduction tree having the premises as initial list and having the conclusion as a line of every path.

Correctness is an easy consequence of the fact that we designed the deduction rules to have this property.

> **Correctness of deduction rules:** If all premises are true in a valuation, all lines in at least one list of conclusions will be true in that same valuation.

Then every statement appearing in every *path* must be true in each valuation in which all initial lines are true, and so the inference from those lines to that statement is valid.

Completeness is best proved by showing how to convert a *standard* reduction tree for an inference into a deduction tree with the premises as initial list and with the conclusion as a line of every path. A standard reduction tree is defined as a closed tree in which the denial of the conclusion and its consequences (and theirs, etc.) are the last lines to which rules are applied.

2-6 PROBLEM

Describe a method for converting standard reduction trees into deduction trees, and apply it to Examples 1, 3 to 7, and 10.

TRUTH-FUNCTIONAL EQUIVALENCE

he statement "It is not the case that whales are not mammals" is a roundabout way of saying that whales are mammals. Indeed, the double denial of any statement at all is equivalent to the original statement in this sense:

Statements are said to be equivalent when their truth values agree in all cases.

In particular, statements are said to be truth-functionally equivalent when their truth values agree in all cases as to joint truth and falsity of the ultimate substatements out of which they are formed by means of truth-functional connectives.

Example 1: The Law of Double Denial
The result of writing two dashes before a statement is equivalent to the original statement. Proof: as denial reverses truth value in each case, double denial gives back the original truth value in each case.

Example 2: All Valid Statements Are Equivalent

Proof. As all valid statements are true in all cases, their truth values must agree in all cases. Thus, "Cows fly or not" is equivalent to "Tomorrow it will rain or not."

Example 3: All Unsatisfiable Statements Are Equivalent

Proof. Their truth values (viz., f) agree in all cases. Thus, "Min is but is not on board" is equivalent to "Tomorrow it will rain but it will not."

The following fact is noteworthy:

Equivalence comes to the same thing as mutual implication.

Proof. The counterexamples to the hypothesis that each of two statements implies the other are precisely the cases in which they have different truth values.

3-1 VENN DIAGRAMS

It is useful to picture logical relationships among statements as relationships among sets of cases in which those statements are true. In the simplest situations the number of possible cases is finite (2^n different truth valuations of n different statement letters), but it is easy enough to imagine situations in which there are infinitely many different letters and hence infinitely many different valuations. Thus, in the statements

$$-(A_1 \,\&\, -A_2) \qquad -(A_2 \,\&\, -A_3) \qquad -(A_3 \,\&\, -A_4) \qquad \ldots$$

appear all letters in the endless sequence

$$A_1 \qquad A_2 \qquad A_3 \qquad A_4 \qquad \ldots$$

so that a case would be determined by an endless sequence of truth values, e.g., one case is determined by assigning

$$t \qquad f \qquad t \qquad f \qquad \ldots$$

to the successive A's so that A_i is true or false depending on whether i is odd or even.

Now let us represent the various truth valuations of statement letters by the points in a rectangle. All tautologies will have the same set of t cases, represented by the whole rectangle, and all unsatisfiable statements will have the same (empty) set of t cases. Any other statement will have some intermediate set of t cases, represented by some region intermediate between the full rectangle and the null "region." See Figure 3-1: if the points in the circle represent the t cases for some statement p, then the rest of the points in the rec-

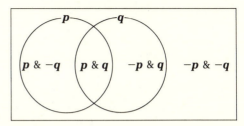

Figure 3-1   Figure 3-2

tangle represent the f cases for **p**, i.e., the t cases for −**p**. (And the points in the circle represent the f cases for −**p**, i.e., the t cases for − −**p**, as required by the law of double denial.)

Representing the t cases for two statements **p**, **q** by the points in two overlapping circles within the rectangle in Figure 3-2, we find that the t cases for the conjunction **p** & **q** are represented by the points common to the **p** and **q** circles, i.e., the points in their lens-shaped intersection, while the disjunction **p** ∨ **q** has as its t cases the points in the union or merger of the two circles, i.e., the lens **p** & **q** together with the lune **p** & −**q** (the points in **p** but not in **q**) and the lune −**p** & **q** (the points not in **p** but in **q**).

We can now read various laws of equivalence off the diagram, using the fact that statements are equivalent when their t cases are represented by the same region of the diagram, and only then. (Having the same t region, they will have a common f region as well, i.e., the rest of the rectangle outside the common t region.)

Example 4: Equivalent Pairs

No matter what statements **p** and **q** may be, the following pairs are equivalent.

p	(**p** & −**q**) ∨ (**p** & **q**)	(law of expansion)
p ∨ (−**p** & **q**)	**p** ∨ **q**	(law of absorption)
−(**p** ∨ **q**)	−**p** & −**q**	(De Morgan's law)
−(**p** & **q**)	−**p** ∨ −**q**	(De Morgan's other law)
p & **q**	**q** & **p**	(commutative law)
p ∨ **q**	**q** ∨ **p**	(commutative law)

Proofs.   Law of expansion: the **p** circle is made up of the lune **p** & −**q** together with the lens **p** & **q**. Law of absorption: the merger of the **p** circle with the lune −**p** & **q** is the same region as the merger

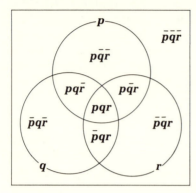

Figure 3-3

of the **p** and **q** circles. De Morgan's law: the t cases for $-(p \lor q)$ are represented by the region outside the merger of the two circles, i.e., the region labeled "$-p$ & $-q$." De Morgan's other law: the region outside the lens is the merger of the regions outside the two separate circles.

Observe that De Morgan's laws allow us to distribute the dash over the terms of a disjunction or a conjunction only after changing wedges to ampersands or ampersands to wedges: "$-(A \lor B)$" is not equivalent to "$-A \lor -B$," nor is "$-(A \& B)$" equivalent to "$-A \& -B$." Thus, the denial of "Min is home or on board," i.e., idiomatically, "Min is neither home nor on board," is not equivalent to "Min is not home or not on board," but to "Min is not home *and* not on board." Similarly, "Min is not both home and on board" is equivalent to "Min is not home or not on board," *not* to "Min is not home and not on board."

Further laws of equivalence can be verified with the aid of a diagram showing the eight sorts of cases relevant to three statements (Figure 3-3). In labeling the diagram we use abbreviations: ampersands are omitted (so that juxtaposition indicates conjunction) and dashes are written over the letters they deny, e.g., "$-p$ & q & $-r$" becomes "$\bar{p}q\bar{r}$."

Example 5: Associative and Distributive Laws
No matter what statements **p**, **q**, and **r** may be, the following triples and pairs are equivalent.

$p \& q \& r$	$(p \& q) \& r$	$p \& (q \& r)$	(associativity of &)
$p \lor q \lor r$	$(p \lor q) \lor r$	$p \lor (q \lor r)$	(associativity of $\lor$)
$p \& (q \lor r)$		$(p \& q) \lor (p \& r)$	(& distributes over $\lor$)
$p \lor (q \& r)$		$(p \lor q) \& (p \lor r)$	($\lor$ distributes over &)

We illustrate the method of verification in the case of the first distributive law. The intersection of the **p** circle with the merger of the other two is the **pqr̄** ∨ **pqr** ∨ **pq̄r** region: the top three bits of the **q** ∨ **r** merger. But that is precisely the merger of the **p** & **q** region (**pqr̄** ∨ **pqr**) with the **p** & **r** region (**pqr** ∨ **pq̄r**).

3-2 BLOCK DIAGRAMS

Notice that in the associative laws, **p** & **q** & **r** and **p** ∨ **q** ∨ **r** are treated as results of applying ternary (three-place) connectives to the three statements **p**, **q**, **r**, e.g., we do *not* treat "*A* & *B* & *C*" as an abbreviation of "(*A* & *B*) & *C*" or of "*A* & (*B* & *C*)." Thus, verifying the first associative law is a matter of seeing that the central **pqr** region is the part of the **pq** lens that lies inside the **r** circle, and is equally the part of the **p** circle that lies inside the **q** & **r** lens. The difference among the three statements that are found to be equivalent in this way can be seen clearly in their block diagrams (Figure 3-4).

We can think of block diagrams as directions for applying the formation rules of Section 1-7 in various ways to get various statements. Indeed, the boxes may be thought of as mechanisms having statements as inputs and longer statements as outputs, e.g., in the leftmost block diagram above, the "&" box forms an output statement (**p** & **q** & **r**) out of input statements **p**, **q**, **r**.

But we can also think of block diagrams as representing circuits of the sorts used in digital computing machines. Arrows represent wires that can be at either of two voltage levels: a low voltage f (say, 0 volts) or a higher voltage t (say, 1 volt). "&" boxes are voltage minimizers: the output is the same as the lowest input, so that the

Figure 3-4

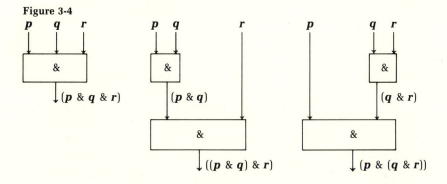

output is high (t) if all inputs are, and is low (f) if even one input is. "∨" boxes are voltage maximizers: the output is the same as the highest input, so that the output is low (f) if all inputs are, and is high (t) if even one input is. Finally, "−" boxes are voltage inverters: the output is high/low if the input is low/high. Identifying t = 1 and f = 0, we have this:

$$p_1 \& p_2 \& \ldots \& p_n = \min(p_1, p_2, \ldots, P_n)$$
$$p_1 \vee p_2 \vee \ldots \vee p_n = \max(p_1, p_2, \ldots, p_n)$$
$$-p = 1 - p$$

Now laws of equivalence can be used to simplify circuits. For instance, according to the law of absorption, the inverter and minimizer are not needed in the more complicated of the circuits shown in Figure 3-5 because the two are equivalent in the sense that their outputs agree in voltage whenever all corresponding inputs do. Circuits will be equivalent in that sense if, and only if, the corresponding statements are equivalent in the sense that their truth values agree in all cases.

We have seen that ampersands and wedges can function as n-place connectives for n = 2, 3, . . . ; the corresponding boxes have n inputs. And the dash is a one-place connective. This suggests the question, "Are there any zero-place connectives, for which the corresponding boxes have outputs but no inputs at all?" The answer is "Yes": there are two zero-place connectives, viz., "t" and "f." Electrically, the output of a t box would be a wire at a constant 1-volt level, and the output of an f box would be a wire at a constant 0-volt level. As statements, "t" and "f" are the shortest tautology and the shortest unsatisfiable statement: in every case the first is true and the second is false.

If you don't have a t box, you can make one out of an inverter and a maximizer as in Figure 3-6. No matter whether point p is high or low, one of the inputs to the maximizer will be high, so that its output can be relied upon to be high. In terms of statements, $p \vee -p$ is a tautology (whatever p may be), and so it is equivalent to "t." To make an f box instead, replace the maximizer by a minimizer: $p \& -p$ is equivalent to "f." But neither electrically nor logically need we think of t and f as constructed out of other items. Rather, "t" and "f" are the basic constants, and they enter directly into laws of equivalence.

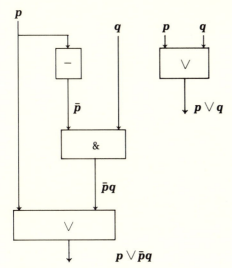

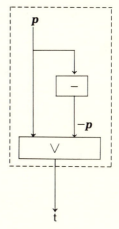

Figure 3-6   t box.

Figure 3-5

3-3   PROBLEMS

1. *Laws of cancellation.* Use the "Euler" diagram shown in Figure 3-7 to explain why:

   (a) If **p** implies **q**, then **p** & **q** is equivalent to **p**.

   (b) If **p** implies **q**, then **p** ∨ **q** is equivalent to **q**.

   Explain why c to e are special cases of a and b.

   (c) f & **q** is equivalent to f.

   (d) **p** ∨ t is equivalent to t.

   (e) t & **p**, f ∨ **p**, and **p** are equivalent to each other.

   Then explain c to e directly, in terms of a diagram consisting simply of a **p** circle inside a square.

2. Simplify the circuits shown in Figure 3-8a, b, and c, i.e., find simplest equivalent block diagrams.

3. Give brief verbal explanations of the following facts.

   (a) *Transitivity of equivalence:* If **p** is equivalent to **q** and **q** is equivalent to r, then **p** is equivalent to **r**.

   (b) If **p** is equivalent to **q**, then −**p** is equivalent to −**q**.

Figure 3-7   Problem 1.

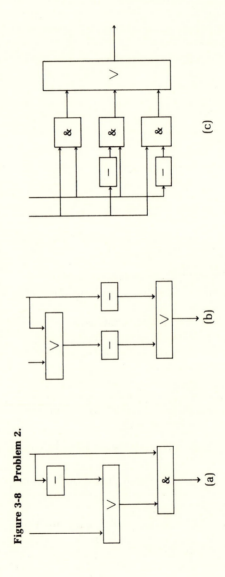

Figure 3-8 Problem 2.

4. Use diagrams or laws of equivalence to simplify the following statements as much as you can, i.e., find simplest-seeming statements equivalent to the given ones.
   (a) Either Moriarty and Crun are both guilty or Crun is innocent (= not guilty).
   (b) Either Crun is guilty or both he and Moriarty are.
   (c) Either Moriarty is guilty or he and Crun are innocent.
   (d) Moriarty is guilty or Crun is innocent or both are guilty.
   (e) They are not both guilty, and at least one is innocent.
   (f) Either both are guilty or Moriarty is but Crun is not.
   (g) They are both guilty or both innocent, and at least one of them is guilty.
   (h) They are not both guilty or not both innocent.

5. Do the same for these.
   (a) Either Holmes is right and the vile Moriarty is guilty, or he is wrong and the scurrilous Crun did the job; but those scoundrels are either both guilty or both innocent.
   (b) Crun is innocent, but either Holmes is right or Crun and Moriarty are both guilty.
   (c) Crun is guilty, and either Holmes is right or Crun and Moriarty are both guilty or both innocent.

6. *Duality.* The "dual" of a statement in which "−," "&," and "∨" are the only connectives is formed by replacing "&" by "∨" and "∨" by "&" throughout. Explain the following fact.

Law of duality: If two statements are equivalent, so are their duals.

3-4 EXPRESSIVE COMPLETENESS

Denial, conjunction, and disjunction are not the only connectives for which we might have introduced special notation. Others are the *Sheffer stroke* connectives "|" (*nand*) and "↓" (*nor*), where "$A \mid B$" means *not both A and B* and "$A \downarrow B$" means *neither A nor B*:

A	B	$A \mid B$	$A \downarrow B$
t	t	f	f
t	f	t	f
f	t	t	f
f	f	t	t

Another is the ternary connective "[, ,]," where "[*A*, *B*, *C*]" means *A if B, C if not* and agrees in truth value with "*A*" or with "*C*," depending on whether "*B*" is true or false:

A	*B*	*C*	[*A*, *B*, *C*]
t	t	t	t
t	t	f	t
t	f	t	t
t	f	f	f
f	t	t	f
f	t	f	f
f	f	t	t
f	f	f	f

Other important examples are the truth-functional conditional and biconditional of Chapter 4, and further examples of less general interest arise in considering particular problems.

But none of this additional notation is strictly necessary, for the dash, ampersand, and wedge suffice to express all truth functions whatever:

Denial, conjunction, and disjunction form an expressively complete set of truth-functional connectives.

This means that for each of the $2^{(2^n)}$ different ways of assigning t or f to each of the 2^n different truth valuations of n different statement letters, there is a statement compounded out of those letters by means of denial, conjunction, and disjunction that has the given assignment as its truth table. Thus, any "new" truth-functional compound such as "[*A*, *B*, *C*]" will prove to be equivalent to some statement built out of statement letters, dashes, ampersands, wedges, and parentheses.

The thing is easy to see. Each truth valuation of a finite set of letters can be described by a conjunction of some of those letters (i.e., those true in the valuation) with a conjunction of denials of the rest (i.e., those false in the valuation). As an example, consider a valuation of six letters, with the corresponding conjunction written in abbreviated notation:

Letters:	*ABCDEF*
Valuation:	t f f t f t
Conjunction:	$A\bar{B}\bar{C}D\bar{E}F$

The conjunction is true in the valuation it describes (of the given letters) and false in all others. Now, given any truth table for a satisfiable truth function, we can write out a disjunction having that as its truth table. This will be the complete disjunctive normal form:

> **Complete disjunctive normal form:** A disjunction of the conjunctions describing the t cases of the given truth table.

Example 6: The Sheffer Strokes

The table for *nand* $(A \mid B)$ has t cases tf, ft, ff for AB, so the complete disjunctive normal form is "$A\bar{B} \vee \bar{A}B \vee \bar{A}\bar{B}$." For *nor* $(A \downarrow B)$ there is just one t case (ff for AB), so the "disjunction" has only one term, "$\bar{A}\bar{B}$." So we have these equivalences:

(a) $A \mid B$, $(A \& -B) \vee (-A \& B) \vee (-A \& -B)$

(b) $A \downarrow B$, $-A \& -B$

Example 7: The Bracket Notation

As the t cases are ttt, ttf, tft, fft for "$[A, B, C]$," the complete disjunctive normal form is "$ABC \vee AB\bar{C} \vee A\bar{B}C \vee \bar{A}\bar{B}C$."

Example 8: Disjunction

As the t cases for "$A \vee B$" are tt, tf, ft, the complete disjunctive normal form is "$AB \vee A\bar{B} \vee \bar{A}B$." (Of course "$A \vee B$" is simpler, and equivalent.)

One possibility remains to be considered: that in which the statement for which a complete disjunctive normal form is sought is unsatisfiable, so that there are no t cases. Here we can use "f" as the complete disjunctive normal form. (We could equally well use "$A \& -A$" or "$B \& -B$," to show that denial, conjunction, and disjunction always suffice—together with statement letters and parentheses—to express any truth function; the zero-place connectives "t" and "f" are not needed. But, having noticed that, it is simplest to use "f.")

Not all three of "$-$," "$\&$," and "$\vee$" are needed in order to express all truth functions, for De Morgan's laws and the law of double denial allow us to replace either of the last two by the other together with denial. For *n*-place conjunctions and disjunctions the relevant equivalences are:

$$p_1 \& p_2 \& \ldots \& p_n \qquad -(-p_1 \vee -p_2 \vee \ldots \vee -p_n)$$

(De Morgan's laws)

$$p_1 \vee p_2 \vee \ldots \vee p_n \qquad -(-p_1 \& -p_2 \& \ldots \& -p_n)$$

But the associative laws allow us to make do with the case $n = 2$: to prove expressive completeness of a certain set of connectives, we need only (1) prove the equivalence with "$-A$" of some statement all of whose connectives belong to that set, and (2) prove the equivalence either with "$A \& B$" or with "$A \lor B$" of some other statement all of whose connectives belong to the set.

Example 9: Expressive Completeness of "Nand"

The set consisting of " | " alone is expressively complete. Proof: as is easily verified by truth tables, "$(A \mid A)$" is equivalent to "$-A$," and "$(A \mid B) \mid (A \mid B)$" is equivalent to "$A \& B$."

Although it is a routine matter to verify the two equivalences cited in Example 9, discovering them is another matter, requiring some thought, e.g., as follows. Reflect that "$A \mid B$" means the same as "$-(A \& B)$." Then "$-(A \mid B)$" will be equivalent to "$-\,-(A \& B)$," i.e., to "$A \& B$." Then we've got it if we can define "$-A$" in terms of "nand." Well, "$A \mid A$" means the same as "Not both A and A," i.e., "$-(A \& A)$." But that is equivalent to "$-A$," so we are finished.

Here we have used the fact that "$A \& A$" is equivalent to "A," i.e., in Latinate jargon, the fact that conjunction is *idempotent* (*idem* = "same," *potens* = "power"). Similarly, disjunction is idempotent, i.e., these three are equivalent:

$$p \qquad p \& p \qquad p \lor p \qquad \text{(laws of idempotence)}$$

In contrast, observe that *nand* is not idempotent: "$A \mid A$" is not equivalent to "A."

To prove that a set of connectives is *not* functionally complete, we must prove that some truth functions (at least one) cannot be defined in terms of connectives in the set.

Example 10: t Cannot Be Defined in Terms of & and $\lor$

(Neither can f; nor can $-$.) The claim is that there are no tautologies among statements in which no connectives but conjunction and disjunction appear. The claim is true because conjunction and disjunction have this characteristic: *when all components p_i are false, so are the conjunction $p_1 \& \ldots \& p_n$ and the disjunction $p_1 \lor \ldots \lor p_n$.* Then no compound using only those two connectives will be true in the valuation where all statement letters are false, and thus no such compound can be a tautology, true in *all* valuations.

3-5 PROBABILITIES AGAIN

We now formulate some general rules for computing probabilities of statements in terms of probabilities of other statements. The first four rules may be taken as axioms (called the "Kolmogorov axioms" after A. N. Kolmogorov).

K0 Equivalent statements have equal probabilities.
K1 Probabilities are nonnegative real numbers.
K2 Valid statements have probability 1.
K3 If two statements are not jointly satisfiable, the probability of their disjunction is the sum of their separate probabilities.

In understanding such rules it is useful to think of probabilities of statements as areas of the regions of Venn diagrams that represent the sets of cases in which those statements are true. Thus K0 is obvious, since equivalent statements have exactly the same t cases, and K3 corresponds to the fact that where regions do not overlap, their total area is simply the sum of their individual areas. K1 corresponds to a natural assumption, that areas are nonnegative real numbers; and K2 requires us to use the full rectangle as the unit of area.

The business of formulating such rules as K3 in words soon becomes tiresome, e.g., the diagrammatically obvious rule that the area of $p\overline{q}$ is what remains of the area of p when the lens pq is removed (Figure 3-9) is muddy in plain English: "The probability of the conjunction of one statement with the denial of an other is the probability of the one minus the probability of its conjunction with the other." Then we formulate such rules in an obvious notation (with "c" for "chance" or for "credence," depending on whether you interpret probability objectively or subjectively):

K0 $c(p) = c(q)$ if p and q are equivalent

K1 $c(p) \geqslant 0$

K2 $c(p) = 1$ if p is valid

K3 $c(p \lor q) = c(p) + c(q)$ if $p \mathbin{\&} q$ is unsatisfiable

K4 $c(p \mathbin{\&} -q) = c(p) - c(p \mathbin{\&} q)$

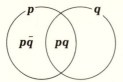

Figure 3-9

It is instructive to derive laws like $K4$ from the axioms $K0$ to $K3$, even though such laws are best understood in diagrammatic terms (e.g., Figure 3-9). Here is a proof of $K4$ in compact form, with numbers under "=" signs indicating the rules that justify the equations: $c(p) \overset{=}{0} c(p\bar{q} \vee pq) \overset{=}{3} c(p\bar{q}) + c(pq)$. In such proofs, the equation between the first and last expressions is the indicated rule, except for minor algebraic manipulations. Here are more rules and their derivations from the axioms. (The reader should verify them also in diagrammatic terms.)

$K5 \quad c(p \vee q) = c(p) + c(q) - c(p \,\&\, q)$

Proof.
$c(p \vee q) \overset{=}{0} c(p\bar{q} \vee q) \overset{=}{3} c(p\bar{q}) + c(q) \overset{=}{4} c(p) - c(p \,\&\, q) + c(q)$.

$K6 \quad c(-p) = 1 - c(p)$

Proof. $\quad 1 \overset{=}{2} c(p \vee -p) \overset{=}{3} c(p) + c(-p)$.

$K7 \quad c(p) = 0 \quad$ if p is unsatisfiable.

Proof. $\quad 1 \overset{=}{2} c(-p) \overset{=}{6} 1 - c(p)$.

$K8 \quad c(p) \leqslant c(q) \quad$ if p implies q.

Proof. $\quad c(q) \overset{=}{0} c(p \vee \bar{p}q) \overset{=}{3} c(p) + c(\bar{p}q) \overset{\geqslant}{1} c(p)$.

$K9 \quad 0 \leqslant c(p) \leqslant 1$.

Proof. $\quad 0 \overset{\leqslant}{1} c(p) \overset{\leqslant}{8} c(t) \overset{=}{2} 1$.

Finally we note the following rule.

K10. The improbability of the conclusion of a valid inference is at most the sum of the improbabilities of its premises:

$c(-q) \leqslant c(-p_1) + \cdots + c(-p_n) \quad$ if $p_1, \ldots, p_n$ together imply q.

(The improbability of a statement is the probability that it is false, i.e., the probability that its denial is true.) $K10$ warns us that where premises are numerous, e.g., as in the lottery paradox of Section 1-5, even near certainty about each of them is compatible with rejection of the conclusion. Two special cases of $K10$ are especially transparent.

Example 11: One-Premise Inferences

If the inference from p to q is valid, all t cases for the premise are t cases for the conclusion as well, so that in Figure 3-10 the area *outside* the outer, q circle (the *improbability* of the conclusion) falls short by $c(-p \ \& \ q)$ of the area outside the inner, p circle (the improbability of the premise). Thus we have $c(-q) \leqslant c(-p)$ when p implies q.

   Proof. $c(-q) \overset{=}{\underset{6}{}} 1 - c(q) \overset{\leq}{\underset{8}{}} 1 - c(p) \overset{=}{\underset{6}{}} c(-p)$.

Example 12: Inference to the Conjuction of Two Premises

Graphically (see Figure 3-11), the improbability of $p_1 \ \& \ p_2$ is the sum $a_2 + a_3 + a_4$ of the areas of the regions outside the lens, whereas the sum of the improbabilities $a_3 + a_4$ of p_1 and $a_2 + a_4$ of p_2 is $a_2 + a_3 + 2a_4$. Thus $c(-(p_1 \ \& \ p_2)) \leqslant c(-p_1) + c(-p_2)$.

   Proof.
   $c(-(p_1 p_2)) \overset{=}{\underset{0}{}} c(\bar{p}_1 \vee \bar{p}_2) \overset{=}{\underset{5}{}} c(\bar{p}_1) + c(\bar{p}_2) - c(\bar{p}_1 \bar{p}_2) \overset{\leq}{\underset{1}{}} c(\bar{p}_1) + c(\bar{p}_2)$.

Figure 3-10
$K10$ with $n = 1$.

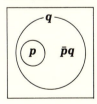

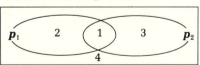

Figure 3-11   Inference to the conjunction of two premises.

3-6 PROOF BY MATHEMATICAL INDUCTION

Although we can easily prove certain special cases of $K10$ as in Examples 11 and 12 above, proof of $K10$ in full generality requires a more powerful method, viz., mathematical induction. This is a method of proving that all members of an infinite sequence $s_1, s_2, \ldots$ of statements are true by proving that

("Basis")   the first member is true

and that

("induction step")   if an arbitrary member s_n is true, then so is the next, s_{n+1}

The induction step is conveniently viewed as a matter of deducing the conclusion s_{n+1} from the "inductive hypothesis" s_n.

In our inductive proof of $K10$, s_n is the statement that $K10$ is true of all inferences with n premises:

(s_n)   The improbability of the conclusion of any valid inference *with* *n premises* is at most the sum of the improbabilities of the premises.

Here is the proof.

Basis. s_1, which makes the claim s_n about one-premise inferences, was proved in Example 11 above.

Induction step. From the inductive hypothesis s_n above we wish to deduce the conclusion

(s_{n+1}) $c(-q) \leqslant c(-p_1) + c(-p_2) + \ldots + c(-p_{n+1})$ if (I) is valid

where (I) is the inference with $n + 1$ premises indicated below:

p_1
p_2 $p_1 \,\&\, p_2$
.   .
.   .
.   .
$\underline{p_{n+1}}$ $\underline{p_{n+1}}$
q q
(I)   (II)

Now observe that if (I) is valid, so is the n-premise inference (II) beside it. Applying the inductive hypothesis to (II), we have

(*) $c(-q) \leq c(-(p_1 \mathbin{\&} p_2)) + \cdots + c(p_{n+1})$ if (I) is valid

Now in Example 12 we proved that $c(-(p_1 \mathbin{\&} p_2)) \leq c(-p_1) + c(-p_2)$. Combining this inequality with (*), we have the conclusion s_{n+1}.

This completes an inductive proof of $K10$. The method is one we have already used informally in the proofs of correctness in Section 2-4.

Warning. Mathematical induction is a conclusive method of deductive proof. It should not be confused with the inconclusive nondeductive methods (also called "inductive") that Francis Bacon, David Hume, J. S. Mill, and many others have characterized roughly and variously as constituting the method of the empirical sciences: the "inductive" sciences, as they are sometimes called. A standard example of this nondeductive, inconclusive sort of induction is the inference that Europeans are said to have made from the premise

All the swans we have seen have been white

to the tentative conclusion

All swans are white

—and to have withdrawn upon finding black swans in Australia. We might call that process "empirical induction," to give it a name of its own. Whatever its merits, it is an entirely different process from mathematical induction, i.e., what we call simply "induction" or "inductive proof" in this book.

3-7 PROBLEMS

1. Find complete disjunctive normal forms for these:
   (a) $(A \mathbin{\&} B) \vee C$ (b) $A \mathbin{\&} B$ (c) $-(A \mathbin{\&} B)$ (d) $[f, A, t]$

2. For each of these, identify a simple statement using only familiar connectives ($-$, $\mathbin{\&}$, $\vee$) with the same Venn diagram.
   (a) $A \downarrow A$ (b) $(A \downarrow B) \downarrow (A \downarrow B)$ (c) $(A \downarrow A) \downarrow (B \downarrow B)$
   (d) $[-A, -B, -B]$ (e) $[A, B, C]$

3. Prove that (a) *nor* by itself is expressively complete; (b) so is the pair consisting of the dash and the bracket notation; and (c) so is the trio consisting of "t," "f," and the bracket notation.

4. Use an underlined wedge "$\underline{\vee}$" for exclusive disjunction, with this truth table:

p	q	$p \underline{\vee} q$
t	t	f
t	f	t
f	t	t
f	f	f

(a) Is $\underline{\vee}$ commutative?
(b) Is $\underline{\vee}$ associative?
(c) How would you define $(p_1 \underline{\vee} \ldots \underline{\vee} p_n)$? (Write out appropriate truth conditions in English.)

5. (a) Is $\underline{\vee}$ idempotent?
(b) Define f in terms of $\underline{\vee}$.
(c) Define $-$ in terms of $\underline{\vee}$ and t.
(d) Prove that $\underline{\vee}$, &, and t together are expressively complete.

6. Find a law that does for $\underline{\vee}$ what K5 does for $\vee$. Prove it.

7. The probabilities that Min is home and that Hen is are each .90. Prove that the probability that they are both home cannot be less than .80 or more than .90. (Suggestion: apply K10 to the inference from p, q to p & q, and to the inference from p & q to p.)

8. What can we conclude about the probability that either Min is not home or she is on board, if the probability is .80 that she is home, but only .70 that she is on board?

9. Prove by induction the following generalization of K3:

K11   The probability of an n-termed disjunction is the sum of the probabilities of the terms, provided the conjunction of any two terms has probability zero: $c(p_1 \vee \ldots \vee p_n) = c(p_1) + \cdots + c(p_n)$ provided $c(p_i \& p_j) = 0$ whenever $i \neq j$.

---

10. Two statements are said to be (probabilistically) *independent* when the probability of their conjunction is the product of their probabilities. Give an example of a probability assignment c and three statements p_1, p_2, p_3, where each pair of the p's is independent, but $c(p_1 \& p_2 \& p_3) \neq c(p_1)c(p_2)c(p_3)$. (Suggestion: let p_3 be $p_1 \underline{\vee} p_2$, where p_1 and p_2 refer to outcomes of different tosses of a coin.)

3-8 COMPACTNESS

A case in which all statements in a set are true is automatically one in which all statements in any of its subsets are true. Then in particular, *if an infinite set of statements is satisfiable, so is every finite subset.* That is trivially true no matter how we understand "case," i.e., no matter what satisfiability (= truth in some case) amounts to. But its converse is another matter:

Compactness theorem: A set of statements s_1, s_2, ... is truth-functionally satisfiable if each finite subset is.

(Note: the whole set counts as one of its own subsets, so if the whole set is finite, there is nothing to prove.) In proving this theorem we use the fact that in truth-functional logic, cases are valuations in which each statement letter can be assigned t or f independently of the values assigned to any or all other letters. (At the end of this book we encounter *second-order* logic, in which "case" means something different enough so that the corresponding concept of satisfiability lacks the compactness property. Truth-functional logic is of 0th order!)

Let r_1, r_2, ... be an infinite sequence of statement letters containing all letters occurring in the various s's. And let us arrange the various truth valuations of the first n statement letters (for $n = 0, 1, 2, \ldots$) in the form of a family tree, as shown in Figure 3-12.

Each node of this *valuation tree* represents a truth valuation of some initial segment of the sequence of letters r_i, e.g., the node "ttf" represents the valuation assigning t to r_1 and r_2 and assigning f to r_3. In general, nodes at level n represent the 2^n distinct truth valuations of the first n letters, and the two immediate descendants

Figure 3-12   Valuation tree.

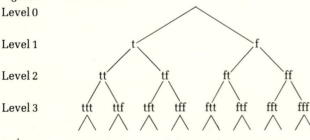

Level 0

Level 1

Level 2

Level 3

of each such node represent the two ways of extending that valuation to the next letter r_{n+1}. Any complete (unending) path through the tree represents a valuation of the whole sequence of r's.

Given particular statements $s_1, s_2, \ldots$, we *prune* the valuation tree by deleting each node that represents a truth valuation falsifying any of the s's. Of course, when we drop a node in that way, we also drop all its descendants, for each of them falsifies all the s's that the parent node falsifies, and perhaps falsifies other s's as well.

Example 14: Pruning the Tree for the Following Sequence

$$-(A_1 \ \& \ -A_2) \qquad -(A_2 \ \& \ -A_3) \qquad -(A_3 \ \& \ -A_4) \ldots$$

Here the ith letter r_i is "A" with subscript i, and $s_i = -(r_i \ \& \ -r_{i+1})$. Starting with $i = 1$, the nodes at level $i + 1$ represent valuations of $r_1, \ldots, r_i, r_{i+1}$ of which one-fourth falsify s_i. These are the nodes ending "tf," i.e., those that assign t to $r_i \ \& \ -r_{i+1}$. They are the right-hand immediate descendants of nodes at level i that end in "t." Deleting such nodes and all their descendants, we have the pruned tree shown in Figure 3-13, consisting of the rightmost path in the original tree (all nodes in which "t" never appears) together with all the leftmost of the paths in the original tree that start from nodes in that rightmost path.

Call a tree infinite" if it has infinitely many nodes. To prove the compactness theorem we use König's lemma:

König's lemma: An infinite tree in which each node has only finitely many immediate descendants must have an infinite branch.

(In our pruned valuation trees, each node has 0 to 1 or 2 immediate descendants.)

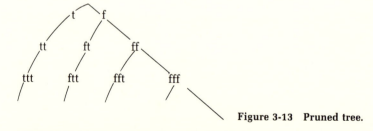

Figure 3-13 Pruned tree.

Proof of König's lemma. We continue to speak in terms of family trees, with each node being the head of the family consisting of its immediate descendants (if any) together with theirs (if any) and so on. Call a node "fit" (as in the phrase "survival of the fit") if the family it heads is infinite, and call a node "unfit" if the family it heads is finite (and thus eventually dies out). Because each node has only a finite number of immediate descendants, we have this situation:

If each immediate descendant of a node is unfit, so is that node.

Or we can put the same matter the other way around:

A fit node has at least one fit immediate descendant.

Now suppose infinite a tree in which each node has only finitely many immediate descendants. To prove König's lemma we specify a path through that tree, and prove that it has no last node. Of course, the first node in the path is the top node of the tree—a node that is fit by hypothesis, as the tree is infinite. Being fit, that node has at least one fit immediate descendant. Let the second node in the path be the leftmost of those. Since that node is fit, too, it will also have a fit immediate descendant. And so on. At stage n in this procedure we are at a fit node that must therefore have at least one fit immediate descendant, and we specify the $n + 1$'st node in the path as the leftmost of those. At every stage in the construction of this path we can take one more step, as a fit node always has a fit immediate descendant (and *finitely* many, so that there will surely be a leftmost of them). Then the path is unending, and König's lemma is proved (by mathematical induction! Identify *basis* and *induction step*).

Our proof of the compactness theorem uses one more lemma.

Pruning lemma: If each finite subset of the s's is satisfiable, the pruned valuation tree must be infinite.

Proof. (From the assumption that the pruned tree is *finite*, we deduce the existence of an *un*satisfiable finite subset Q of the s's.) If the pruned tree is finite, then for some sufficiently large n, no node of level n appears in it, i.e., each of the 2^n valuations of

$r_1, \ldots, r_n$ falsifies at least one s. For each such valuation, choose the earliest member of the sequence $s_1, s_2, \ldots$ that it falsifies. Let Q be the set of all such earliest members. Now Q is a finite subset of the s's, for it contains no more than 2^n statements. And it is unsatisfiable: each valuation of $r_1, \ldots, r_n$ makes some member of Q false. The lemma is proved.

Combining the two lemmas, we find that

> If each finite subset of the s's is satisfiable, then there is an infinite path P through the pruned valuation tree.

To prove the compactness theorem, it only remains to notice that

> In the valuation of the r's that is determined by an infinite path through the pruned valuation tree, all the s's are true.

(Pruning the tree was a matter of *deleting* nodes representing valuations that falsify any of the s's. If one of the s's had been false in the valuation of $r_1, r_2, \ldots$ represented by an infinite path, it would have been false in the valuation of $r_1, \ldots, r_n$ corresponding to the nth node in that path, where $r_1, \ldots, r_n$ include all the statement letters in that s. Then the path could not have been infinite; it would have stopped before level n.) Conclusion:

> If each finite subset of the s's is satisfiable, so is the whole set.

That is the compactness theorem.

Note that the compactness theorem can be reformulated in either of these ways:

> Every truth-functionally unsatisfiable set of statements has a truth-functionally unsatisfiable finite subset.
>
> Any conclusion truth-functionally implied by a set of premises is truth-functionally implied by a finite subset of those premises.

(As any set counts as one of its own subsets, these claims are trivial unless the sets they refer to are infinite.)

CHAPTER 4

CONDITIONALS

I s the conditional "if . . . then" construction represented by one of the 16 two-place truth-functional connectives? If so, then (as we shall see) there can be no doubt of which one it is: the truth-functional conditional can only be the connective symbolized by the arrow "→" in the survey of all two-place truth functions shown in Figure 4-1. (The other new connective is the double arrow "↔," viz., the truth function that most closely resembles the ordinary *biconditional* "if and only if." Note that this is the denial of the underlined wedge "$\underline{\vee}$" that was introduced in Section 3-7 for exclusive disjunction.)

Discussion of conditionals has been so far delayed not because of any complexity in the truth functions → and ↔, but rather because it *seems* clear that many of the most important uses of conditionals in everyday talk and thought defy truth-functional analysis; the closest truth function, →, appears not to be close enough to serve some of our most important purposes in using conditionals. And if this appearance is deceptive (and we shall examine an argument to that effect below), some analysis will be required of the non-truth-functional idioms that we had thought ourselves to have been using in our conditional statements. Here logic impinges upon some of the oldest problems of philosophy.

fftt	p
ftft	q
tttt	t
tttf	$p \mid q$
ttft	$p \to q$
ttff	$-p$
tftt	$q \to p$
tftf	$-q$
tfft	$p \leftrightarrow q$
tfff	$p \downarrow q$
fttt	$p \vee q$
fttf	$p \veebar q$
ftft	q
ftff	$-p \,\&\, q$
fftt	p
fftf	$p \,\&\, -q$
ffft	$p \,\&\, q$
ffff	f

Figure 4-1   The two-place truth functions. (Denials are situated symmetrically above and below the broken line.)

4-1   THE PHILONIAN CONDITIONAL

The dispute between advocates of the truth-functional account of conditionals and the advocates of other, more complex but seemingly more adequate accounts is as old as logic itself. The truth-functional account is first known to have been proposed by Philo of Megara ca. 300 B.C., in opposition to the view of his teacher, Diodorus Cronus. We know of this through the writings of Sextus Empiricus some 500 years later, the earlier documents having been lost. According to Sextus,

> Philo says that a sound conditional is one that does not begin with a truth and end with a falsehood. ... But Diodorus says it is one that neither could nor can begin with a truth and end with a falsehood.*

* William Kneale and Martha Kneale, *The Development of Logic,* Oxford University Press, 1962, pp. 128–129.

There can be no doubt that what Sextus refers to is precisely the truth-functional connective that we have symbolized by the arrow, for he says elsewhere,

> So according to him there are three ways in which a conditional may be true, and one in which it may be false. For a conditional is true when it begins with a truth and ends with a truth, like "If it is day, it is light"; and true also when it begins with a falsehood and ends with a falsehood, like "If the earth flies, the earth has wings"; and similarly a conditional which begins with a falsehood and ends with a truth is itself true, like "If the earth flies, the earth exists." A conditional is false only when it begins with a truth and ends with a falsehood, like "If it is day, it is night."*

So Sextus reports Philo as attributing truth values to conditionals just as in our table for →, except for the order in which he lists the cases:

p	q	$p \rightarrow q$
t	t	t
t	f	f
f	t	t
f	f	t

We shall want to see why this (if any) is the right truth table for "if . . . then," and we shall want to compare the merits of the truth-functional account with those of some of its rivals. But first let us note some correspondences between English and logical notation.

"$A \rightarrow C$" goes over into English as well (or as poorly) as any of these:

If A then C If A, C C, if A

In the last two readings the comma may be omitted where it is not needed in order to make the intended grouping clear. In each of the three English versions, as in the version with the arrow, "A" is called the *antecedent* of the conditional and "C" is called the *consequent*. Observe that in the three English versions *the antecedent is always the statement following the word "if"*—even in the third version, where the antecedent comes after the consequent! This flexibility

---

* Kneale and Kneale, op. cit., p. 130.

in position of the antecedent is used in English to avoid the awkward double "if" that would result from unvarying use of the "if . . . then" form in conditionals with conditional antecedents, as in

If if we advance then they withdraw then we'll win.

In arrow notation this would be

(We advance → They withdraw) → We'll win

Idiomatic English separates the "if"s by using the "C if A" form for the inner conditional or for both conditionals:

If they withdraw if we advance then we'll win.

We'll win, if they withdraw if we advance.

The comma is needed for clarity in the second of these. Without it, the whole could be misread as a version of

We advance → (They withdraw → We'll win)

To say *that* in idiomatic English, move the comma:

We'll win if they withdraw, if we advance.

4-2 NON-TRUTH-FUNCTIONAL CONDITIONALS

All the foregoing conditionals are in the indicative mood; antecedents and consequents are declarative sentences or are conditionals having such sentences as *their* antecedents and consequents. It is only for such conditionals that the truth-functional interpretation has any plausibility. (Note, by the way, that it is only declarative sentences that are ordinarily spoken of as true or false.) In sharp contrast are *counterfactual* conditionals, which are often formulated in the subjunctive mood.

Example 1: Philonian and Counterfactual Conditionals*

(1) If Oswald did not kill Kennedy, someone else did.

(2) If Oswald had not killed Kennedy, someone else would have.

Surely the first of these is true (*someone* killed Kennedy), but the second is probably false. Then a single analysis will not do for both.

All conditionals are partly truth-functional: where the antecedent proves true and the consequent false, the conditional statement is refuted. Thus the credentials of line 2 of our truth table are impeccable:

p	q	If p then q
t	t	?
t	f	f
f	t	?
f	f	?

Now for some conditionals, that is all there is to the truth table. It is not that such conditionals have no truth values at all when their antecedents are false or their consequents true, but that in such cases different conditionals can assume different truth values, and (as shown in the following examples) a single conditional can assume one truth value or the other depending on extraneous conditions. So it would seem, anyway.

Example 2: A Causal Conditional?
Gravely, my dentist says, "If you continue to neglect that tooth, you'll lose it," i.e., "If N then L." Except in the tf case for NL, the compound statement seems capable of assuming either truth value, depending on circumstances. The title of this example is a query because one might agree that belief in a causal process leading from neglect to loss is what led the dentist to make his conditional statement and yet deny that existence of such a causal link is any part of what he *asserts* by making that statement. Thus in the second tt case of the table shown in Figure 4-2, one might think that the dentist was actually right, and the conditional *true*, by luck: right for the wrong reason.

* This example is from Ernest Adams, "Subjunctive and Indicative Conditionals," *Foundations of Language* 6:89–94, 1970.

N L	Under these conditions, the conditional has this value:	
t t	Neglect continues, an abscess bursts, and the tooth must be extracted.	t
	Neglect continues; the tooth is knocked out accidentally and proves to have been quite sound.	f
t f	Neglect continues, but the tooth serves lifelong.	f
f t	After receiving professional attention, the tooth is knocked out accidentally. Unattended, and with no accident, it would have been lost through decay.	t
	After receiving professional attention, the tooth is knocked out accidentally. But the attention was pointless: the tooth was perfectly sound all along.	f
f f	At the eleventh hour, needed attention saves the tooth, which remains serviceable lifelong.	t
	Attended to unnecessarily, the tooth nevertheless remains sound and serviceable lifelong.	f

Figure 4-2 A causal conditional?

Example 3: "Strict Implication"

There is an extreme point of view in which conditionals are seen as true or false depending on whether or not their antecedents logically *imply* their consequents. Here it is clear that in cases 1, 3, and 4, mere truth values of antecedent and consequent do not determine the truth value of the whole conditional. Use the fish-hook "$\dashv$" for this sense of "if ... then." It is called "strict implication." In the table shown in Figure 4-3, the upper conditionals in the tt and ff cases are true because any statement (true or false) implies itself, and the lower conditionals there are false for the same reason that the inference from "*A*" to "*B*" is invalid. In analyzing iterations, e.g.,

Sharks fly $\dashv$ (Whales fly $\dashv$ Whales fly)

notice that for statements with "$\dashv$" as main connective, truth comes to the same thing as validity (true in all cases if true in one), and falsity comes to the same thing as unsatisfiability. Then the conditional displayed above is true, for its consequent is valid.

p q	Conditionals with given truth values of *p*, *q*	$p \dashv\hspace{-0.3em}3\, q$
t t	Sharks swim $\dashv\hspace{-0.3em}3$ Sharks swim	t
	Sharks swim $\dashv\hspace{-0.3em}3$ Whales swim	f
t f	Sharks swim $\dashv\hspace{-0.3em}3$ Whales fly	f
f t	Whales fly $\dashv\hspace{-0.3em}3$ (Whales fly $\vee$ $-$Whales fly)	t
	Whales fly $\dashv\hspace{-0.3em}3$ Sharks swim	f
f f	Whales fly $\dashv\hspace{-0.3em}3$ Whales fly	t
	Whales fly $\dashv\hspace{-0.3em}3$ Sharks fly	f

Figure 4-3   Strict implication.

4-3   INFERENCES FROM CONDITIONAL PREMISES

As any conditional is false when its antecedent is true and its consequent false, it must be that *any true conditional has a false antecedent or a true consequent*. Then where "→" is any conditional connective (truth-functional, counterfactual, strict, causal, or what have you), we have the rule of inference in Figure 4-4. By adding that to the other tree rules we can test validity of inferences of various familiar forms. The names given below for the various valid forms and fallacies are customary adaptations or abuses of traditional terminology.

$p \rightarrow q$

$-p \mid q$ Figure 4-4   Rule for conditionals.

Example 4: *Modus Ponens* (or "Detachment")

If I neglect it, I'll lose it.	1	$\sqrt{\ } N \to L$	(prem
I neglect it.	2	N	(prem)
I'll lose it.	3	$-L$	(−concl)
	4	$-N \quad L$ $\times \quad \times$	(from 1)

Example 5: *Modulus Tollens*

If I neglect it, I'll lose it.	1	$\sqrt{\ } N \to L$	(prem)
I'll not lose it.	2	$-L$	(prem)
I don't neglect it.	3	$-\,-N$	(−concl)
	4	$-N \quad L$ $\times \quad \times$	(from 1)

Example 6: Fallacy of Denying the Antecedent

If I neglect it, I'll lose it.	1	$\sqrt{\ } N \to L$	(prem)
I do not neglect it.	2	$-N$	(prem)
I'll not lose it.	3	$\sqrt{\ } -\,-L$	(−concl)
	4	L	(from 3)
	5	$-N \quad L$	(from 1)

Counterexample (both paths): the ft case for NL.

Example 7: Fallacy of Affirming the Consequent

If I neglect it, I'll lose it.	1	$\sqrt{\ } N \to L$	(prem)
I'll lose it.	2	L	(prem)
I neglect it.	3	$-N$	(−concl)
	4	$-N \quad L$	(from 1)

Counterexample (both paths): the ft case for NL.

Example 8: Dilemma

I'll attend to it or lose it.	1	$\sqrt{A \lor B}$	(prem)
If I attend to it, it'll hurt now.	2	$\sqrt{A \to C}$	(prem)
If I lose it, it'll hurt later.	3	$\sqrt{B \to D}$	(prem)
It'll hurt now or later.	4	$\sqrt{-(C \lor D)}$	(−concl)
	5	$-C$	(from
	6	$-D$	4)

```
7        -A      C       (from 2)
        / \      ×
8    - B    D            (from 3)
    / \     ×
9   A   B               (from 1)
    ×   ×
```

Lacking a rule for denied conditionals, we are not yet able to come to any conclusion about the validity of certain familiar forms of inference.

Example 9: Contraposition

If I neglect it, I'll lose it.	1	$\sqrt{N \to L}$	(prem)
If I don't lose it, I'll not have neglected it.	2	$-(-L \to -N)$	(−concl)
	3	$-N \quad L$	(from 1)

Both paths are open, but as an unchecked compound statement appears in both, no conclusion can be drawn about validity. (This inference will prove valid on the truth-functional interpretation of "if . . . then.")

Example 10: Fallacy of Conversion

If I neglect it, I'll lose it.	1	$\sqrt{N \to L}$	(prem)
If I lose it, I'll have neglected it.	2	$-(L \to N)$	(−concl)
	3	$-N \quad L$	(from 1)

Again, the unchecked compound statement in both paths blocks either conclusion about validity. (This inference will prove to be invalid on the truth-functional reading of "if . . . then.") Here and in Example 9, the shift in tense from premise to conclusion is a matter of English grammar that has no counterpart in logical notation, where we imagine the period of neglect and the later time of loss as specified in the truth conditions for the tenseless statement letters "N" and "L." In English, the antecedent determines the temporal point of view for the whole conditional: the period of neglect in the premise, and the time of loss in the conclusion. Thus the loss is referred to in the future tense in the premise, while in the conclusion the neglect is referred to in the past tense.

4-4 INFERENCES FROM DENIED TRUTH-FUNCTIONAL CONDITIONALS

Let us now return to our original use of the arrow as a notation for a truth-functional sense of "if . . . then," and ask what its truth table must be. To answer that question we need a guiding principle, e.g., minimality:

> **Minimality:** $(p \to q)$ is the weakest additional premise that allows us to infer q from p.

Rationale. Any sort of conditional statement is an "inference ticket" entitling the bearer to infer the consequent from the antecedent (together with the conditional statement itself). Validity of the ticket is assured as long as "If A, B" is f in the tf case for AB (Figure 4-5). We can then be sure that the conditional will not be true when its antecedent is true and its consequent false: we can be sure that there are no counterexamples to the inference that the ticket is meant to validate. Identifying $\to$ as the *weakest* such connective means that if $\Rightarrow$ is any connective, truth-functional or not, for which the inference ticket is valid, then $p \Rightarrow q$ implies $p \to q$. Thus, $p \to q$

Figure 4-5 Why the ticket is valid.

t	A
	If A then B
	————
f	B

Counterexamples are t cases for the second premise.

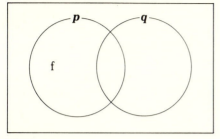

p	q	$p \to q$
t	t	t
t	f	f
f	t	t
f	f	t

Figure 4-7 Truth table for the arrow.

Figure 4-6

is meant to be nothing *but* an inference ticket for getting from p to q.

The weakest statements are the valid ones, i.e., those true in all cases. (To be told that it will or will not rain tomorrow is to be told nothing about the weather.) And in general, one weakens a statement by modifying it so that it will be true in more cases. Thus the weakest statement that is false in the tf case for its successive components is the one that is true in all other cases: $p \to q$. There are eight different truth functions of p, q that are false if p is true and q false, i.e., there are eight different ways of assigning t or f to each of the three unmarked cells of the Venn diagram shown in Figure 4-6. The weakest of these is the one obtained by assigning t to all.

We have now "discovered" the truth table for the arrow: see Figure 4-7. True truth-functional conditionals are those with false antecedents or true consequents. The others are false. Essentially, what we have learned is that the truth-functional conditionals are those for which the second row of the truth table is the *only* f case. Then statements of these three forms are equivalent:

$$p \to q \qquad -p \lor q \qquad -(p \ \& \ -q)$$

And the rule of inference for denied truth-functional conditionals must be as in Figure 4-8.

$$\frac{-(p \to q)}{\begin{array}{c} p \\ -q \end{array}}$$

Figure 4-8 Rule for denied truth-functional conditionals.

$$\frac{N \to L}{-L \to -N}$$

1	$\sqrt{}N \to L$	(prem)
2	$\sqrt{}-(-L \to -N)$	(−concl)
3	$- L$	(from
4	$- - N$	2)
5	$-N \qquad L$	(from 1)
	$\times \quad \times$	

(a)

$$\frac{N \to L}{L \to N}$$

1	$\sqrt{}N \to L$	(prem)
2	$\sqrt{}-(L \to N)$	(−concl)
3	L	(from
4	$- N$	2)
5	$-N \qquad L$	(from 1)

(b)

Figure 4-9   (a) Contraposition: valid. (b) Conversion: invalid.

We can now resolve the questions of validity that were left open in Examples 9 and 10 through lack of a rule for denied conditionals. The trees for contraposition and conversion are shown in Figure 4-9. Example 11 is another question of the same sort.

Example 11: "Syllogism"

$$\frac{\begin{array}{c} A \to B \\ B \to C \end{array}}{A \to C}$$

1	$\sqrt{}A \to B$	(prem)
2	$\sqrt{}B \to C$	(prem)
3	$\sqrt{}-(A \to C)$	(−concl)
4	A	(from
5	$-C$	3)
6	$-B \qquad C$	(from 2)
	$\qquad\quad \times$	
7	$-A \qquad B$	(from 1)
	$\times \qquad \times$	

Without the rule for denied conditionals, the tree would have two open paths with line 3 in each, blocking either conclusion about validity.

4-5 BICONDITIONALS

Where the conditional $p \to q$ and its converse $q \to p$ both hold, we say that the biconditional $p \leftrightarrow q$ holds:

p	q	$(p \to q)$ & $(q \to p)$			$p \leftrightarrow q$
t	t	t	t	t	t
t	f	f	f	t	f
f	t	t	f	f	f
f	f	t	t	t	t

> The biconditional is true/false when its two components agree/disagree in truth value.

Here are the rules of inference:

$$(p \leftrightarrow q)$$

p	$-p$
q	$-q$

$$-(p \leftrightarrow q)$$

p	$-p$
$-q$	q

Each rule has two lists of conclusions, and each list is two lines long. Biconditionals and their denials make for messy trees.

How do they go over into English? Well, "Min's home if and only if Henry is" is a fairly concise way of saying that either they're both home or neither of them is. Thus the double arrow goes over as "if and only if" (or "iff," in mathematicians' shorthand). And as the denied biconditional is true when either component is, *without* the other, the denied double arrow comes to the same thing as the underlined wedge: exclusive disjunction.

Example 12: Conditional Does Not Imply Biconditional

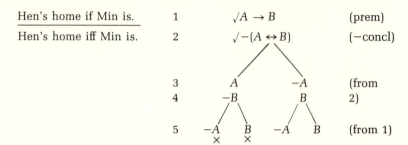

| Hen's home if Min is. | 1 | $\sqrt{}A \rightarrow B$ | (prem) |
| Hen's home iff Min is. | 2 | $\sqrt{}-(A \leftrightarrow B)$ | (−concl) |

3	A $-A$	(from
4	$-B$ B	2)
5	$-A$ B $-A$ B	(from 1)

Both open paths determine the ft case for AB as a counterexample. Note that the conclusion, in full, is "Hen's home if and only if Min is."

Example 13: Biconditional Implies Conditional

Hen's home iff Min is.	1	$\sqrt{}A \leftrightarrow B$	(prem)
Hen's home if Min is.	2	$\sqrt{}-(A \rightarrow B)$	(−concl)
	3	A	(from
	4	$-B$	2)
	5	A $-A$	(from
	6	B $-B$	1)

Example 14: Exclusive "Or" Implies Inclusive

Exactly one is home.	1	$\sqrt{}-(A \leftrightarrow B)$	(prem)
At least one is home.	2	$\sqrt{}-(A \vee B)$	(−concl)
	3	$-A$	(from)
	4	$-B$	2)
	5	A $-A$	(from
	6	$-B$ B	1)

The premise of this inference could equally well have been transcribed into logical notation as "$A \veebar B$" (writing that as line 1 and leaving the rest of the tree as above). The rules for $p \veebar q$ and $-(p \veebar q)$ are the same as those for $-(p \leftrightarrow q)$ and $p \leftrightarrow q$, respectively.

The "if and only if" reading of the double arrow suggests "only if" as a reading of the single arrow in place, after the antecedent and before the consequent. ("If" won't do: p if q corresponds to $p \leftarrow q$, so to speak.) The suggestion is that these are stylistic variants, having identical truth conditions.:

If p then q p only if q q if p

The phrase "only if" serves to label what follows it as a *necessary condition* (*conditio sine qua non*) for what precedes it, as in

You'll succeed only if you try.

Transformation into either of the other forms demands a change of tense, e.g., here:

If you succeed then you will have tried.

Note that while "if" alone preceded the antecedent, "only if" precedes the consequent. On its own, "if" marks what follows it as *sufficient* for truth of the other part, as in

You'll succeed if you try.

This is quite a different statement from the earlier two: putting "only" before "if" has the effect of *conversion*, with the new conditional asserting sufficiency of the condition that the old condition asserted to be necessary. *A propos:* the biconditional, p *if and only if* q, says that truth of p is *necessary* ("if") *and sufficient* ("only if") for truth of q.

Notice one more variant: "unless not" for "if," as here:

You'll succeed if you try.   You'll succeed unless you don't try.

You try → You succeed   −You try $\vee$ You succeed

Thus where the truth-functional reading of "if" is correct, *unless* is a stylistic variant of *or* (in the inclusive sense). The difference between "if" and "unless not" above is the difference in point of view on the relationship between succeeding and trying. In the "if" statement, trying is represented as a way to bring about success—the prediction is withdrawn in case you don't try. (Where you don't try, neither success nor failure is predicted by the "unless not" statement.)

4-6 ASTOUNDING INFERENCES

The truth-functional reading, in which "if . . . then" is a stylistic variant of "not . . . or," is attractively clear and simple, but it seems to conflict with judgments we ordinarily make, in which we reject as invalid certain inferences having valid truth-functional analogs.

Example 15: Hyperbole

I'll have a second cup.	1	S	(prem)
I'll die if I don't have a second cup.	2	$\checkmark -(-S \rightarrow D)$	(−concl)
	3	$-S$	(from
	4	$-D$	2)
		×	

Example 16: True Grit

I'll ski tomorrow.	1	S	(prem)
I'll ski tomorrow if I break my leg today.	2	$\checkmark -(B \rightarrow S)$	(−concl)
	3	B	(from
	4	$-S$	2)
		×	

Example 17: The Conditional or Its Converse Holds

An unlikely tautology: "Either I'll ski tomorrow if I break my leg today, or I'll break my leg today if I ski tomorrow."

1	$\checkmark -((B \rightarrow S) \vee (S \rightarrow B))$	(−concl)
2	$\checkmark -(B \rightarrow S)$	(from
3	$\checkmark -(S \rightarrow B)$	1)
4	B	(from
5	$-S$	2)
6	S	(from
7	$-B$	3)
	×	

Example 18: Zapping Them with Logic*

"We'll win, for if they withdraw if we advance, we'll win; and we won't advance!" That argument is valid on the Philonian reading of "if."

1	$\checkmark(A \rightarrow B) \rightarrow C$	(prem)
2	$-A$	(prem)
3	$-C$	($-$concl)

$$\diagup \quad \diagdown$$

4	$\checkmark-(A \rightarrow B)$ C	(from 1)
	$\times$	
5	A	(from
6	$-B$	4)
	$\times$	

Example 19: If It Works at All, It's Not Fail-Safe

"It explodes if it's armed and fired" implies "Either it explodes if it's armed or it explodes if it's fired," on the truth-functional reading of "if."

1	$\checkmark(A \& B) \rightarrow C$	(prem)
2	$\checkmark-((A \rightarrow C) \vee (B \rightarrow C))$	($-$concl)
3	$\checkmark-(A \rightarrow C)$	(from
4	$\checkmark-(B \rightarrow C)$	2)
5	A	(from
6	$-C$	3)
7	B	(from
8	$-C$	4)

$$\diagup \quad \diagdown$$

9	$-(A \& B)$ C	(from 1)
	$\times$	

$$\diagup \quad \diagdown$$

10	$-A$ $-B$	(from 9)
	$\times$ $\times$	

Of course the validity of the truth-functional versions of these inferences is not in question: since all the trees close, the transcriptions of all these inferences into the arrow notation are valid. But there is serious question of the correctness of those transcriptions *as translations*, simply because the transcriptions really are valid, whereas the English versions seem invalid or, anyway, bizarre.

* Examples 18 and 19 are adapted from Peter Geach, *Reason and Argument*, University of California Press, Berkeley 1976.

It is noteworthy that when "if" is transcribed as "or not," the English versions seem valid (but pointless as inferences). Thus, Example 15 comes out this way (with double denial suppressed, so that "if not" becomes simply "or"):

I'll have a second cup.
_____
I'll die or I'll have a second cup.

Right: if I'll have a second cup, then I'll die (or fly, or anything you care to say) or have a second cup. So what? Similarly, the inference in Example 16 becomes valid but pointless:

I'll ski tomorrow.
_____
I'll ski tomorrow or not break my leg today.

The conclusion could have been "I'll ski tomorrow or break my leg today" or "I'll ski tomorrow or the next day," with equal validity and equal pointlessness. With "or not" in place of "if" there is little tendency to reject the conclusion as imputing a nonexistent connection between the components. If it is rejected at all, the ground is pointlessness, not falsity. But if we then replace "or" by "unless," the conclusion once more seems to assert a connection between its components:

I'll have a second cup.
_____
I'll die unless I have a second cup.

4-7   CONVERSATIONAL IMPLICATURE

The argument that, despite these disparities, "if . . . then" really has the same truth conditions as "not . . . or" has been put most persuasively by those who remind us that mere truth is not the object of discourse. Thus, the disingenuous eyewitness who identifies the culprit as "Tom or Dick" when he saw quite clearly that it was Dick is speaking "the" truth, but a truth calculated to mislead. Why is this truth misleading? Because we rightly expect that when someone provides information by making a statement ("Tom or Dick did it"), there is no relevant shorter and more informative truth ("Dick did it") that he knows. "Dick did it" is *relevant* because it is formed of the same components as the other, and *more informative* because its t cases (tt, ft) are a proper subset of the other's (tt, tf, ft).

Normally in asserting a disjunction there is what Paul Grice calls a "conversational implicature" to the effect that the speaker is not in a position to assert either disjunct alone.* This is not implied by the disjunction actually asserted, but is normally "inferred" as an explanation of the fact that the speaker chose to assert the full disjunction instead of one of its components. That is why inferences of these forms seem pointless, ordinarily:

$$\frac{p}{p \vee q} \qquad \frac{-p}{-p \vee q} \qquad \frac{-p}{p \to q} \qquad \frac{q}{p \to q}$$

The premises are so much simpler and more informative than the conclusions that we are at a loss to know what motive there is for drawing such an inference. Knowing the premise, why not assert it instead of the conclusion? The point is brought out further in the following example.

Example 20: Too Many Premises[†]
The following valid inference loses its *bizarrerie* when the second premise is dropped.

> Either Dr. Adams or Dr. Brown will operate.
> Dr. Brown will not operate.
> ___
> If Dr. Adams does not operate, Dr. Brown will.

Without the second premise, all is well: the conclusion, read truth-functionally, is equivalent to the first premise, and may be seen as a restatement of it in a form appropriate for reassuring someone who fears that Dr. Adams will not be available. But the second premise opens a new route to the conclusion: if Dr. Brown will not operate, then (by the first premise) Dr. Adams will, and we reach the conclusion by the inane step from "A" to "$-A \to B$." But why take that step? Why not simply say that Dr. Adams *will* operate?

Thus defenders of the truth-functional reading of everyday conditionals point out that the disjunction "$-A \vee C$" shares with the conditional "If A then C" the feature that normally it is not to be asserted by someone who is in a position to deny "A" or to assert

---

* Paul Grice, William James Lectures, Harvard University, 1967. (Unpublished, except in small part: "Logic and Conversation," pp. 64–75 of *The Logic of Grammar*, edited by Donald Davidson and Gilbert Harman, Dickenson Publishing Co., Encino and Belmont, California, 1975.)

† From Ernest Adams, "The Logic of Conditionals," *Inquiry*, **8**:166–197, 1965.

"C." Then we are right to object, when someone asserts a conditional because its antecedent is false, or because its consequent is true. The objection (they argue) is not that the speaker cannot be sure the conditional is true in such cases, for he can. The objection is rather that in such cases the speaker can expect the conditional assertion to be misleading or confusing or defective in some other way, *even though true*. Normally, then, conditionals will be asserted only by speakers who think the antecedent false or the consequent true, but know not which. Such speakers will think they know of some connection between the components, by virtue of which they are sure (enough for the purposes at hand) that the first is false or the second is true. Then when my dentist says, "If you continue to neglect that tooth, you'll lose it," there is a *conversational implicature* to the effect that the neglect will cause the loss, but (the argument concludes) existence of such a causal connection is not *implied* by the statement itself, and so lack of such a connection is not enough to falsify the conditional.

So far, so good. But how shall we deal with these examples, if we interpret everyday conditionals as truth-functional?

Example 21: Perils of Foresight

"I'll break my leg today. I know that's true because I know it's false that if I break my leg today, I'll ski tomorrow."

$-(B \to S)$	1	$\checkmark -(B \to S)$	(prem)
B	2	$-B$	(−concl)
	3	B	(from
	4	$-S$	1)
		×	

Example 22: Consolation of Logic

"I won't die before noon. I know that's true because I know it's false that if I don't have a second cup, I'll die before noon."

$-(-C \to D)$	1	$\checkmark -(-C \to D)$	(prem)
$-D$	2	$--D$	(−concl)
	3	$-C$	(from
	4	$-D$	1)
		×	

No matter how well the conversational implicature ploy works as an account of ordinary statements having the form of conditionals overall, it seems not to work for denials of such statements. It seems *false*, and not merely misleading or puzzling, to say "If I break my leg today, I'll ski tomorrow," and therefore it seems true to deny that conditional. But surely truth of that denial is no ground for expecting that I will break my leg today. Thus the English inference in Example 21 seems invalid, while its truth-functional transcription is obviously valid. And the case is the same, essentially, in Example 22. If these appearances are real, then the truth-functional interpretation of "if . . . then" cannot be maintained after all.

The problem we are facing is that of the "other side of the inference ticket"—the minimal ticket allowing the bearer to get from p to q once the bearer has $p \rightarrow q$. Because the ticket is minimal, it has on its other side a ticket entitling the bearer to p and also to $-q$ once the bearer has $-(p \rightarrow q)$. The difficulty is illustrated in Examples 21 and 22, and also as follows.

Suppose I go to a consultant for a second opinion when my dentist tells me that if I continue to neglect that tooth, I'll lose it. After extensive testing, the consultant tells me that my dentist was wrong: it is false that I'll lose it if I neglect it. On the truth-functional interpretation of ordinary conditionals, the consultant can only know that if she knows that I will neglect it and won't lose it. Thus she must be something of a seer, knowing such things as that the tooth won't be knocked out accidentally, if she really has the information implied by her second opinion.

But is this really so strange? Why not say, with the implicaturists, that the consultant was overstating her case when she denied my dentist's conditional statement? All she had good grounds for was a rather different statement, denying the existence in me of a condition that, given continued neglect, would lead to decay and eventual loss of that tooth, *other things being equal*, e.g., provided I live long enough for the process of decay to complete itself, provided I do not lose the tooth accidentally in some other way, etc. That would be the line of those who hold that belief in the existence of such a condition in me was the dentist's reason for making his conditional statement, but was no part of what he *asserted* in making that statement. On that line the issue between my dentist and the consultant concerns the dentist's basis for his first opinion, not the expressed opinion itself, i.e., the conditional "If N then L," which can thus (on that line) be read as "$N \rightarrow L$." Then the consultant's statement is not "$-(N \rightarrow L)$" but this, essentially: "Maybe your dentist is right: maybe you'll lose the tooth if you neglect it. But if you do, it won't be because of any present pathology in the tooth, but through some unforeseeable accident."

Reviewing the astounding inferences of Section 4-6 in this spirit, we find that if the premise of each inference is true, the conclusions of Examples 15 and 16 are not a hyperbole and an expression of iron determination, but trivial truths. And in Examples 17 and 19 the sting is drawn from inevitability of the disjunctive conclusion by lack of inevitability of either disjunct alone. Thus it may be inevitable that the device explodes if armed and fired without its being inevitable that it explodes if armed or inevitable that it explodes if fired. (And it may even be inevitable that it *fails* to explode if armed but not fired or fired but not armed.)

Example 18 illustrates a different sort of trap: the strategist would not believe that we'll win, if they withdraw if we advance, unless he believed that we'll advance. Then although the two premises together do imply the conclusion, and although both premises may in fact be true, the strategist's basis for believing the first premise is undermined by his belief in the second—on the salient interpretation of Example 18 as stated.

Then Grice's implicature ploy seems to work, and the astonishing inferences of this section and Section 4-6 seem explicable on the truth-functional reading of the conditionals in them. Still, there remains the problem of interpreting the causal talk that sets forth (say) the dentist's basis for believing his conditional statement true, and the related causal talk that sets forth the consultant's basis for rejecting the dentist's basis—even though the dentist's conditional itself is not thereby denied, but only said to be unfounded. Then even if such conditionals are truth-functional after all, there remain logical or philosophical problems about related idioms (e.g., concerning causation) that seem clearly non-truth-functional.

4-8   PROBLEMS

1. Test validity by the tree method, and determine all counterexamples.

(a) $\dfrac{\begin{array}{c}A \to (B \to C)\\ A \to B\end{array}}{A \to C}$
(b) $\dfrac{\begin{array}{c}A \to (B \to C)\\ A \to C\end{array}}{A \to B}$
(c) $\dfrac{\begin{array}{c}A \to B\\ A \to C\end{array}}{A \to (B \,\&\, C)}$
(d) $\dfrac{\begin{array}{c}A \to C\\ B \to C\end{array}}{(A \lor B) \to C}$

(e) $\dfrac{B \to (A \to C)}{A \to (B \to C)}$
(f) $\dfrac{A}{(A \to B) \to B}$
(g) $\dfrac{A \to (A \to B)}{A \to B}$
(h) $\dfrac{(A \to B) \to A}{A}$

(i) $\dfrac{(A \to B) \to C}{(A \to C) \to C}$
(j) $\dfrac{(A \to C) \to B}{(A \to B) \to C}$
(k) $\dfrac{(A \to B) \to B}{(B \to A) \to A}$
(l) $\dfrac{-(A \to C)}{A \to -C}$

(m) $\dfrac{A \to -C}{-(A \to C)}$
(n) $\dfrac{A \to -A}{-A}$
(o) $\dfrac{C \to A}{-(A \to C)}$
(p) $\dfrac{-(A \to C)}{C \to A}$

(q) $\dfrac{A \to (B \to C)}{(A \,\&\, B) \to C}$
(r) $\dfrac{(A \,\&\, B) \to C}{A \to (B \to C)}$
(s) $\dfrac{(A \lor B) \to C}{A \to C}$
(t) $\dfrac{A \to C}{(A \lor B) \to C}$

2. In (e) to (t) of problem 1, replace $p \rightarrow q$ by $-p \vee q$, replace $-(p \rightarrow q)$ by $p \ \& \ -q$, and then simplify using the laws of equivalence in Chapter 3 to determine in which cases the premises are *equivalent* to the conclusions.

3. Use the tree method to determine whether this statement is a tautology:

$$(A \rightarrow (B \rightarrow C)) \leftrightarrow ((A \rightarrow B) \rightarrow (A \rightarrow C))$$

Then obtain the same result by applying the method of problem 2 to the two sides of the biconditional.

4. Translate into logical notation, using "$\rightarrow$" for "if ... then," and test validity by the tree method.

(a) If Holmes has bungled or Watson's abroad, Moriarty will escape. Does it follow that Moriarty will escape unless Holmes bungles?

(b) Moriarty will escape only if Holmes bungles. Holmes will not bungle, if Watson's to be believed. Does it follow that if Watson's to be believed, Moriarty will not escape?

(c) If Moriarty has escaped, then either Holmes has bungled or Watson's on the job. Holmes has not bungled unless Moriarty has escaped. Watson's not on the job. Does it follow that Moriarty has escaped if and only if Holmes has bungled?

(d) Moriarty will escape unless Holmes acts. We shall rely on Watson only if Holmes does not act. Does it follow that if Holmes does not act, Moriarty will escape unless we rely on Watson?

5. Is the following argument sound? If not, why not? "This argument is unsound, for its conclusion is false, and it is unsound if it has a false conclusion."

6. Evaluate the following statement:

"A rational man can surely consider (a) to be true, and (b) and (c) false. But if conditionals are truth-functional, his belief system would be inconsistent."*

(a) If Paul lives in Paris, he lives in France.

(b) If Paul lives in London, he lives in France.

(c) If Paul lives in Paris, he lives in England.

7. Discuss the following argument (note Example 11):

If Adams wins the election, Brown will retire to private life.
If Brown dies before the election, Adams will win it.
_____

If Brown dies before the election, he will retire to private life.

8. Show that (a) $\rightarrow$ and $-$ together are expressively complete, as are (b) $\rightarrow$ and f, but that (c) $\rightarrow$ alone is not.

* Adapted from Brian Ellis, *Rational Belief Systems*, Blackwell, Oxford, 1979, p. 61.

4-9 CONDITIONAL PROBABILITY

We define a two-place *conditional probability* function $c(\ /\ )$ in terms of the one-place ("unconditional") probability function $c(\ )$:

$$c(q/p) = \frac{c(p\ \&\ q)}{c(p)} \qquad \text{if}\quad c(p) \neq 0 \tag{C}$$

The slant line "/" plays the role of a comma, separating the arguments of the two-place function. It is no connective. The change that takes place when $c(\ /p)$ replaces $c(\ )$ as one's credence function may be called "conditionalization" on p. The thought is that after one learns that p is true, credence in the shaded region of Figure 4-10 drops to 0, and the p circle becomes the new unit of area. But nothing else changes; in particular, relative sizes of subregions of the p circle remain the same after conditionalization as before.

Here are some easy consequences of definition (C):

K12　Suppose $c(p) \neq 0$. Then (a) $c(q/p) = 1$ if p implies q and (b) $c(q/p) = 0$ if p implies $-q$.

K13　*Multiplicative law:* $c(q\ \&\ r/p) = c(q/p)c(r/q\ \&\ p)$ if $c(p\ \&\ q) \neq 0$.

K14　*Bayes' theorem:* $c(q/p) = c(p/q)\dfrac{c(q)}{c(p)}$ if $c(p) \neq 0 \neq c(q)$.

K15　*Law of compound probability:* $c(q) = c(q/p)c(p) + c(q/-p)c(-p)$ if $0 \neq c(p) \neq 1$.

Conditionalization can be repeated: having conditionalized upon p to get from c to d as in (D) below, we can conditionalize again, on q, to get from d to e as in (E):

$$d(r) = c(r/p) \tag{D}$$

$$e(r) = d(r/q) \tag{E}$$

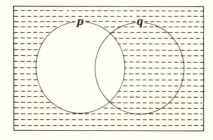

Figure 4-10

Now it is straightforward to verify the following:

K16. The result of successive conditionalization on two statements is the same as that of conditionalizing once on the conjunction of those statements: $e(r) = c(r/p \& q)$ provided $c(p \& q) = 0$.

Proof: $e(r) = d(r/q) = d(r \& q)/d(q) = c(r \& q/p)/c(q/p) =$
$$\quad\;\; \text{E} \qquad\quad \text{C} \qquad\qquad\quad \text{D} \qquad\qquad\qquad \text{C}$$
$c(r \& q \& p)/c(q \& p) = c(r/q \& p) = c(r/p \& q).$
$$\qquad\quad \text{C} \qquad\qquad\qquad 0$$

Example 23: Coin Tossing

If h_i is the statement that the ith toss of a certain coin yields *head*, the usual credence function c assigns equal values to the four cases regarding h_1 and h_2. If we learn that at least one of the first two tosses yielded *head*, it is appropriate to replace c by d as our credence function, with $p = h_1 \vee h_2$ in (D), so that credence in *head on the second toss* changes from $c(h_2) = 1/2$ to $d(h_2) = c(h_2/h_1 \vee h_2) = 2/3$. If we then learn that the two tosses were not both heads, it is appropriate to conditionalize again, replacing d by e as our credence function, with $q = -(h_1 \& h_2)$ in (E), so that credence in h_2 becomes $e(h_2) = d(h_2/-(h_1 \& h_2)) = c(h_2/(h_1 \vee h_2) \& -(h_1 \& h_2)) = 1/2$ again
$$\qquad\qquad\qquad\qquad\qquad\quad 16$$
(see Figure 4-11).

It is instructive to compare the unconditional probability of the truth-functional conditional $p \to q$ with the conditional probability of q on p: see K17.

K17. $c(p \to q) = c(p)c(q/p) + c(-p)1$ if $c(p) \neq 0$

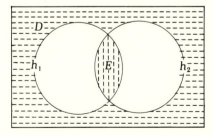

Figure 4-11

There the probability of the conditional is expressed as a weighted average of $c(q/p)$ and 1, the weights being the probabilities $c(p)$ and $c(-p)$ that the antecedent is true and false, respectively. Thus where the antecedent is a near certainty, the probability of the truth-functional conditional is close to the corresponding conditional probability, but where the antecedent is improbable, the probability of the conditional (near 1) reveals nothing about the conditional probability.

Clearly the condition probability $c(q/p)$ cannot generally be identified with the probability $c(p \to q)$ of the corresponding truth-functional conditional, but one might imagine that some non-truth-functional interpretation of "if" might be found for which we can prove the equality of $c(q/p)$ with $c(q$ if $p)$ under very general conditions, e.g., perhaps whenever $c(p) \neq 0$. One could then treat the slant line "/" as a connective ("if"), and one could make sense of such inscriptions as "$c((q/p)/r)$," just as one can make sense (but a different sense) of such inscriptions as "$c(r \to (p \to q))$."

But as David Lewis has shown, there is no hope of that.* Here is a version of his argument in which we assume that if "$c((q/p)/r)$" makes sense, it must represent the result of conditionalizing twice, on p and on r, so that by K16 we have $c((q/p)/r) = c(q/p \ \& \ r)$.

If $(q/p)/r$ makes sense as a statement to which c can be applied, then we have $c(q/p) \stackrel{15}{=} c((q/p)/q)c(q) + c((q/p)/-q)c(-q) \stackrel{16}{=} c(q/p \ \& \ q)c(q) + c(q/p \ \& \ -q)c(-q) \stackrel{12}{=} 1c(q) + 0c(-q) = c(q))$, provided $c(p \ \& \ q) \neq 0 \neq c(p \ \& \ -q)$. Thus by (C) we have $c(p \ \& \ q) = c(p)c(q)$, and we have proved a version of Lewis's trivialization result:

K18. We can treat "/" as a connective only at the cost of finding that whenever $c(p \ \& \ q)$ and $c(p \ \& \ -q)$ are both positive, p and q are *independent* in the sense that $c(p \ \& \ q) = c(p)c(q)$.

Then unless c is so trivial a probability function as to make practically all statements independent of each other, "/" is no connective but a mere typographical variant of a comma that separates the arguments of the two-place conditional probability function.

---

* See his "Probabilities of Conditionals and Conditional Probabilities," *Philosophical Review*, **85**:297–315, 1976.

Example 24: Two Tosses of a Coin

Even in so simple a case as ordinary coin-tossing (Example 23), we cannot treat "/" as a connective, for with $p = h_1 \vee h_2$ and $q = h_2$, both $c(p \,\&\, q)$ and $c(p \,\&\, -q)$ are positive (viz., 1/2 and 1/4) but p and q are not independent, for $c(p \,\&\, q)$ is 1/2, whereas $c(p)c(q)$ is only 3/8.

Lewis's result can be put in an especially striking form as follows.

LEWIS'S TRIVIALIZATION RESULT

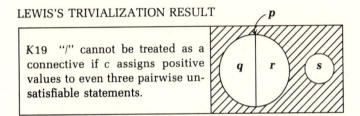

K19 "/" cannot be treated as a connective if c assigns positive values to even three pairwise unsatisfiable statements.

Proof. Let q, r, s be three such statements, and let p be the disjunction $q \vee r$. (See the Euler diagram, where the shaded region may have probability 0, but the unshaded regions have positive probabilities.) Then we have

$$c(p \,\&\, q) \underset{0}{=} c(q) \qquad c(p \,\&\, -q) \underset{0}{=} c(r)$$

both of which are positive by hypothesis. Now by K18, "/" cannot be treated as a connective unless we have $c(p \,\&\, q) = c(p)c(q)$, i.e., $c(q) = c(p)c(q)$, i.e. (dividing by $c(q)$, which is positive by hypothesis), $c(p) = 1$, i.e., by K6, $c(-p) = 0$, which is impossible because $c(s) \underset{8}{\leq} c(-p)$, where $c(s)$ is positive by hypothesis.

C H A P T E R 5

FIRST-ORDER LOGIC

e know that Alma is at home or at work, and then we learn that she is not at home. What can we conclude? By the methods of truth-functional logic we can draw the obvious conclusion that she is at work. But by using new methods, new kinds of conclusions can be drawn, e.g., the conclusion that she does not work at home: home $\neq$ workplace.

5-1 IDENTITY

If we write "*Ah*" for Alma is at home" and "*Aw*" for "Alma is at work," the two inferences under discussion can be represented as in Examples 1 and 2.

Example 1: Old Inference

$Ah \lor Aw$	1	$\sqrt{Ah} \lor Aw$	(prem)
$-Ah$	2	$-Ah$	(prem)
Aw	3	$-Aw$	(−concl)
	4	$Ah \quad Aw$	(from 1)
		$\times \quad \times$	

Example 2: New Inference

$$Ah \lor Aw$$
$$\underline{-Ah}$$
$$-h = w$$

1	$\checkmark Ah \lor Aw$	(prem)	
2	$-Ah$	(prem)	
3	$\checkmark - -h = w$	(−concl)	
4	Ah $\quad$ Aw	(from 1)	
	$\times$		
5	$h = w$	(from 3)	
6	Ah	(from 4, 5)	
	$\times$		

In Examples 1 and 2 we have analyzed atomic statements into parts smaller than statements: place names "h" and "w" and the predicate letter "A" for "Alma is at." In the old inference the patterns "Aw" and "Ah" are treated as if they were unitary statement letters, but in applying the tree method to the new inference, we split the first of these (line 4) into subatomic parts "A" and "w," then replace "w" by "h," and finally reassemble the parts to get the second atom (line 6).

To get line 6 from lines 4 and 5, we used this rule:

RULE FOR IDENTITY

If an open path contains a full line of form $m = n$ and also a full line p in which one of the names m, n appears one or more times, write at the bottom of the path a statement q obtained by replacing some or all of the occurrences of that name in p by the other name, provided q does not already occur in that path as a full line:

$$m = n$$
$$\underline{p}$$
$$q$$

The thought is that if m and n really are one and the same ($m = n$), then anything true of one of them must be true of the other as well: q must be true if obtained from a truth p by substituting equals for equals. To put the same matter the other way around, if something has a characteristic and something lacks it, the things must be distinct. Thus in Example 2, her *workplace* had the characteristic of being where Alma was, while *home* lacked that charac-

Aw	Alma is at work.
$-Ah$	She is not at home.
$w \neq h$	She does not work at home.

Figure 5-1 **If something has a characteristic and something lacks it, the things must be distinct.**

teristic. It followed that the two places were distinct: see Figure 5-1. Similarly, in the following example, the suspicion that the Baron and the Count are really the same man is refuted by the news that the Baron, but not the Count, has the characteristic of being loved by Alma.

Example 3: Leibniz's Law

Alma loves the Baron.	aLb
Alma does not love the Count.	$-aLc$
The Baron is not the Count.	$b \neq c$

1	aLb	(prem)	p
2	$-aLc$	(prem)	
3	$\surd - -b = c$	(−concl)	
4	$b = c$	(from 3)	$m = n$
5	aLc	(from 1, 4)	q
	×		

In the conclusion, "$b \neq c$" abbreviates "$-b = c$." Thus the denial of the conclusion would be written out in full as in line 3 of the tree.

Example 4: Symmetry

If Lewis Carroll (c) is identical with Charles Dodgson (d), then Dodgson is also identical with Carroll.

Carroll is Dodgson.	$c = d$	1	$c = d$	(prem)	$m = n$
Dodgson is Carroll.	$d = c$	2	$d \neq c$	(−concl)	p
		3	$d \neq d$	(from 1, 2)	q
			×		

Line 3 comes from lines 1 and 2 by the rule for identity that was introduced above. But to close the tree we must invoke a new rule, for diversity, $\neq$, i.e., for denied identity:

RULE FOR DIVERSITY

Close any path that contains a line of form $n \neq n$:

$$n \neq n$$
$$\times$$

Example 5: Self-Identity

"Alma is Alma" is a valid statement, true in every case. (There is no need to know who she is to know that she is self-identical!) To test that statement's validity by the tree method, we start a tree with its denial:

1	$a \neq a$	($-$concl)
	$\times$	

By the new rule for diversity, the tree closes immediately, thus certifying "$a = a$" as valid.

Example 6: Transitivity

Here, line 4 of the tree abbreviates the statement "$-a = b$," i.e., the denial of line 1. That is why the tree closes.

$a = b$	1	$a = b$	(prem)
$b = c$	2	$b = c$	(prem)
$a = c$	3	$a \neq c$	($-$concl)
	4	$a \neq b$	(from 2, 3)
		$\times$	

Example 7: Intransitivity

This tree shows that the inference in Example 6 would become invalid if identity were replaced by diversity throughout:

$a \neq b$	1	$a \neq b$	(prem)
$b \neq c$	2	$b \neq c$	(prem)
$a \neq c$	3	$\checkmark -- a = c$	(−concl)
	4	$a = c$	(from 3)
	5	$b \neq a$	(from 2, 4)
	6	$c \neq b$	(from 1, 4)
	7	$a = a$	(from 4, 4)
	8	$c = c$	(from 4, 4)
	9	$c = a$	(from 4, 8)

In generating the path we never came to a line of form $n \neq n$ or to a pair of lines of form p, $-p$, and so in order to finish the tree *we had to keep applying rules of inference until no new statements were forthcoming.* As the finished tree is open, the inference must be invalid—if the tree method for truth functions and identity is complete and correct, with the rules that we now have. (One can prove that it is.) Observe that to get lines 7 and 8 we applied the two-premise rule for identity in a form where the second premise was a repetition of the first:

4	$a = c$	$m = n$		4	$a = c$	$m = n$
4	$a = c$	p		4	$a = c$	p
7	$a = a$	q (p, with m for n)	8	$c = c$	q (p, with n for m)

Nothing in the statement of the rule for identity said that the premises $m = n$ and p had to be different.

5-2 UNIVERSALITY

Little more can be done with identity until we combine it with the device of generalization, as in the song:

> Everybody loves my baby
> But my baby don't love nobody but me.*

---

* "Everybody Loves My Baby," words and music by Jack Palmer and Spencer Williams, MCA Music, New York, 1924. See page iv for complete copyright information.

These two lines make an unexpectedly strong statement: they imply that everybody loves the singer! We shall construct a tree for that inference presently, in Example 12. Meanwhile, let us draw a less remote conclusion from the same premises.

Example 8: Universal Instantiation

| Everybody loves baby. |
| Baby loves nobody but me. |
| Baby is me. |

Logic	$\forall$	L	b	a
English	For all	loves	baby	me

1	$\forall x \ xLb$	(prem)
2	$\forall x \ (bLx \rightarrow x = a)$	(prem)
3	$b \neq a$	(−concl)
4	bLb	(from 1)
5	$\sqrt{(bLb \rightarrow b = a)}$	(from 2)
6	$-bLb \qquad b = a$	(from 5)
	× ×	

The first premise, "$\forall x \ xLb$," is formed by *universally generalizing* the condition "xLb," i.e., "x loves baby"; writing the *universal quantifier* "$\forall x$" before it, we have a statement saying that *everybody* satisfies the condition. A more wooden translation of that statement from logical notation back into a sort of interlingua between Logic and English (sc., "Loglish") appears here (first line):

$\forall x \ xLb$	For all x, x loves baby.
$\forall x \ (bLx \rightarrow x = a)$	For all x, if baby loves x then x is me.
$b = a$	Baby is me.

| Logic | Loglish |

Loglish is almost English; it would be a dialect of English if it did not use variables ("x," in this example) to do jobs of cross-reference that English does differently (with pronouns). We shall have more to say about that later. Meanwhile let us see how the tree method handles universal quantification in the transitions from line 1 to 4 and from line 2 to 5, above.

In Logic and in Loglish, the variable "x" ranges over some *domain*: some nonempty set, identified in English by the choice of pronouns (here, "everybody" and "nobody") together with contextual clues. In Example 8 the pronouns make it clear that the domain is some set of *people*. In any example, it is understood that *all names refer to members of the domain* over which the variables range, so that here, *a* and *b* (me and baby) belong to the domain: they are allowable values of "x." Then "∀x xLb" says, among other things, that *bLb*, and so line 4 comes from line 1 by "universal instantiation": line 4 says about *b* what line 1 says about *everything* in the domain. Similarly, line 5 says about *b* what line 2 says about everything in the domain. Thus line 5 comes from line 2 by universal instantiation.

Here is the rule, stated for any variable *v*:

UNIVERSAL INSTANTIATION (UI)

Given a full line of form ∀*v* *p*[*v*] in an open path: (1) If a name *n* appears in the path, write *p*[*n*] at the bottom unless that statement already appears as a full line of that path. (2) If no names appear in the path, choose some name *n* and write *p*[*n*] at the bottom. When you apply this rule, do *not* check the line ∀*v* *p*[*v*].

$$\frac{\forall v\, p[v]}{p[n]}$$

In Example 8 we used the rule twice, as follows.

1	∀x xLb	$\dfrac{\forall v\, p[v]}{}$	2	∀x (bLx → x = a)	$\dfrac{\forall v\, p[v]}{}$
4	bLb	*p*[*n*]	5	(bLb → b = a)	*p*[*n*]

In both applications the variable *v* was "x" and the name *n* was "b." The two applications differed in regard to the condition *p*[*v*]:

p[ ] = " Lb"   *p*[ ] = "(bL → = a)"

In each case we got *p*[*v*] and *p*[*n*] by writing "x" and "b" in the blanks:

p[*v*] = "xLb"   *p*[*v*] = "(bLx → x = a)"

p[*n*] = "bLb"   *p*[*n*] = "(bLb → b = a)"

Part 1 of the rule requires us to keep writing **p[n]** at the bottom of the path for all names n that appear in the path, as long as the path remains open. It is because we may need to apply UI more than once to the same line that we do not check the line when applying this rule. (Checking a line is equivalent to erasing it.)

Example 9: Applying UI Twice to the Same Line

The Baron loves all who love Alma.
Alma loves herself.

The Baron loves himself.

1	$\forall x\ (xLa \rightarrow bLx)$	(prem)
2	aLa	(prem)
3	$-bLb$	($-$concl)
4	$\sqrt{}aLa \rightarrow bLa$	(from 1)
5	$-aLa$ bLa	(from 4)
6	$\sqrt{}bLa \rightarrow bLb$	(from 1)
7	$-bLa$ bLb	(from 6)

Part 2 of the rule requires us to "make up" a name for use in universal instantiation, in case no names yet appear in the path.

Example 10: Joint Satisfiability

If "Gx" means that x is a griffin and "Hx" means that x is hairy, then two extreme hypotheses about griffins are expressible as in lines 1 and 2 of the following tree, which tests their joint satisfiability:

All griffins are hairy.
No griffins are hairy.

1	$\forall x\ (Gx \rightarrow Hx)$	
2	$\forall x\ (Gx \rightarrow -Hx)$	
3	$\sqrt{}Ga \rightarrow Ha$	(from 1)
4	$\sqrt{}Ga \rightarrow -Ha$	(from 2)
5	$-Ga$ Ha	(from 3)
6	$-Ga$ $-Ha$ $-Ga$ $-Ha$	(from 4)
	1 2 3	

	Ga	Ha
Path 1:	f	
Path 2:	f	f
Path 3:	f	t

Cases in which all full lines in open paths are true.

Line 3 comes from line 1 by part 2 of the rule UI. With the name "a" now in the path, line 4 can come from line 2 by part 1. As not all paths in the finished tree are closed, the set consisting of the two hypotheses is seen to be satisfiable. Path 1 specifies the general case in which the two hypotheses about griffins are jointly true: it is the case in which there are no griffins (so that all the griffins that there are have any attribute you care to mention, e.g., hairiness, nonhairiness, or whatever).

Observe that the restriction at the end of part 1 prevents us from applying UI so as to repeat a full line that is already in the path.

Example 11: An Invalid Statement

If all love Alma, Alma does not love herself.

1	$\sqrt{}-(\forall x\ xLa \rightarrow -aLa)$	
2	$\forall x\ xLa$	(from 1)
3	$\sqrt{}--aLa$	(from 1)
4	aLa	(from 3)

Here we never apply UI, for as "a" and no other name appears in the path, application of UI (to line 2) would have yielded a fifth line that merely duplicated line 4. Observe that line 1 is of form $-(p \rightarrow q)$: there was no question of applying UI to *it*.

5-3   EXISTENCE

The condition "xLb" can be generalized in two different ways: universally, as in "Everybody loves my baby," or existentially, as in "Somebody loves my baby." Having symbolized the universal generalization by "$\forall X\ XLb$," where the rotated "A" suggests "all," we now symbolize the existential generalization by "$\exists x\ xLb$," where the rotated "E" suggests "exists": "$\exists x\ xLb$" goes over into Loglish as "There exists an x such that x loves baby," i.e., there exists *at least* one x such that x loves baby. Thus the existential generalization "$\exists x\ xLb$" is true if in the domain there are one or more who satisfy the condition "xLb," and is false if none do.

For definiteness, imagine that the range of "x" consists of exactly these people: me (a), my baby (b), and Crun (c). Then the universal generalization "$\forall x\ xLb$" has the same truth value as the conjunction "aLb & bLb & cLb," and the existential generalization "$\exists x\ xLb$" has the same truth value as the disjunction "$aLb \lor bLb \lor cLb$": the conjunction/disjunction is true iff all/some members of the domain satisfy the condition "xLb." Thus "∀x" and "∃x" work rather like conjunction and disjunction. In particular, they satisfy versions of De Morgan's laws:

$-\forall x\ xLb$	$-(aLb\ \&\ bLb\ \&\ cLb)$	$-aLb \lor -bLb \lor -cLb$	$\exists x\ -xLb$
$-\exists x\ xLb$	$-(aLb \lor bLb \lor cLb)$	$-aLb\ \&\ -bLb\ \&\ -cLb$	$\forall x\ -xLb$

Then "$-\forall x$" can be rewritten equivalently as "$\exists x-$," and "$-\exists x$" can be written equivalently as "$\forall x-$":

RULE FOR DENIED QUANTIFICATION	
If a statement beginning with $-\forall v$ (or $-\exists v$) occurs as a full line of an open path, check it and write at the bottoms of all open paths in which that line occurs the same statement with $\exists v-$ in place of $-\forall v$ (or with $\forall v-$ in place of $-\exists v$) at the front.	$\sqrt{-\forall v\ p}$ $\exists v - p$
	$\sqrt{-\exists v\ p}$ $\forall v - p$

Examples: "Not everyone loves baby" comes to the same thing as "(There exists) someone (who) doesn't love baby," and denying "Someone loves baby" comes to the same thing as asserting that everybody fails to love baby, i.e., *nobody* loves baby.

We shall need only one more rule of inference: the rule used to get from line 7 to line 8 of the following tree.

Example 12: Existential Instantiation

Everybody loves baby.	1	$\forall x\ xLb$	(prem)
Baby loves nobody but me.	2	$\forall x\ (bLx \rightarrow x = a)$	(prem)
Everybody loves me.	3	$\sqrt{-\forall x\ xLa}$	(−concl)
	4	bLb	(from 1)
	5	$\sqrt{bLb \rightarrow b = a}$	(from 2)
	6	$-bLb \quad b = a$	(from 5)
		$\times$	
(7 Someone doesn't love a)	7	$\sqrt{\exists x\ -xLa}$	(from 3)
(8 Call that someone "c")	8	$-cLa$	(from 7)
	9	cLb	(from 1)
	10	cLa	(from 6, 9)
		$\times$	

In line 7 we are assured of the existence of *someone* in the domain who satisfies the condition "−xLa." If we give that person a name (say, "c") that has not yet been used for anyone in the story, we beg no questions about his or her identity and characteristics. Perhaps "c" is an alias for one of the characters already met: b, perhaps, or a. But equally well, "c" may name some quite new character, not previously met under that or any other name. The crucial fact is that truth of line 7 assures us that *some* interpretation of "c" (as naming a member of the domain) will make true the new line, 8, that we get from 7 by this rule:

EXISTENTIAL INSTANTIATION (EI)

Given an unchecked full line of form $\exists v\, p[v]$ in an open path, inspect the path to see whether it contains a full line of form $p[n]$. If not, choose a name n *that has not been used anywhere in the path* and write the statement $p[n]$ at the bottom. When this has been done for every open path in which the full line $\exists v\, p[v]$ appears, check that line:

$$\sqrt{\exists v\, p[v]}$$
$$p[n]$$

new!

In applying this rule it is absolutely essential that the name n be new to the path. There is no such restriction on universal instantiation, where old names are used wherever possible.

5-4 PROBLEMS

1. Symbolize a to c and test their validity by the tree method. Where the inference is invalid, indicate a counterexample that is determined by an open path on the model shown in Figure 5-2.

   (a) Alma is gregarious.

   Someone is gregarious.

   (b) Someone is gregarious.

   Alma is gregarious.

   (c) All are gregarious.

   Alma is gregarious.

(d) Alma is gregarious. Ga

     All are gregarious. $\forall x\, Gx$

	1	Ga	(prem)
	2	$\checkmark -\forall x\, Gx$	(−concl)
	3	$\checkmark \exists x\, -Gx$	(from 2)
	4	$-Gb$	(from 3)

Figure 5-2 Problem 1.

2. Test validity by the tree method. To which of the four trees is this table relevant?

L	a	b	c
a		f	
b			
c		t	

Explain briefly.

(a) Alma does not love the Baron. $-aLb$

     Not everyone loves the Baron. $-\forall x\, xLb$

(b) Alma does not love the Baron. $-aLb$

     No one loves the Baron. $-\exists x\, xLb$

(c) Everyone loves Alma.

     Alma loves herself.

(d) Everyone loves Alma.

     Alma loves someone.

3. Test validity by the tree method.

(a) Alma loves all who love her. $\forall x\, (xLa \rightarrow aLx)$

     She does not love the Baron. $-aLb$

     He does not love her. $-bLa$

(b) Alma loves herself. aLa

     Alma loves some who love her. $\exists x\, (xLa\ \&\ aLx)$

(c) Alma loves some who love her. $\exists x\, (xLa\ \&\ aLx)$

     She loves none but the Baron. $\forall x\, (aLx \rightarrow x = b)$

     He loves her if she loves him. $aLb \rightarrow bLa$

(d) Not everyone loves Alma, for she loves all who love her, but does not love everyone.

4. By the tree method, test equivalence of a and b, and c and d. Use tables to describe any counterexamples.
   (a) Alma does not love all her lovers. $-\forall x\ (xLa \rightarrow aLx)$
   (b) Alma has a lover whom she does not love. $\exists x\ (xLa\ \&\ -aLx)$
   (c) All who are loved by Alma love her. $\forall x\ (aLx \rightarrow xLa)$
   (d) If Alma loves all, all love her. $\forall x\ aLx \rightarrow \forall x\ xLa$

5. Use the tree method to demonstrate equivalence of these two ways of saying that Alma is no fool:

   $$-\exists x\ (Fx\ \&\ a = x) \qquad\qquad -Fa$$

   Do the same for these two ways of saying that no fool plays chess:

   $$-\exists x\ (Fx\ \&\ Px) \qquad \forall x\ (Fx \rightarrow -Px)$$

6. Use the tree method to test validity of this (fallacious) inference:

   > Alma's no fool.
   > No fool plays chess.
   > ――――――――――
   > Alma plays chess.

   Use a circle diagram to identify the counterexample that the tree determines.

7. In Example 8, we never had to use the rules of inference for identity or diversity. This means that the inference would have been no less valid if in it the sign of identity had been replaced by any other two-place predicate symbol, e.g., "P" for *pays*, as in the following inference. *Work out the tree for this inference:*

   > $\forall x\ xLb$
   > $\forall x\ (bLx \rightarrow xPa)$
   > ――――――――――
   > bPa

8. Applying the foregoing treatment to Example 12, we find that the new inference is invalid. By filling in these two tables, describe the counterexample determined by the leftmost open path in the tree for this inference:

P	a	b	c		L	a	b	c
-----	-----	-----	-----		-----	-----	-----	-----
a					a			
b					b			
c					c			

9. As we all understand the lyrics on first hearing them, the singer does not mean to include baby in the scope of the "everybody" who (he assures us) loves her. On that understanding, the first premise in Example 8 goes over into logical notation as "Everybody *other than baby* loves baby," and the inference becomes invalid:

$$\forall x \, (x \neq b \to xLb)$$
$$\underline{\forall x \, (bLx \to x = a)}$$
$$b = a$$

(a) Test validity by the tree method, and identify all counterexamples that are determined by open paths in the finished tree.

(b) In terms of conversational implicature, explain why "Everybody other than baby loves baby" sounds as if it implies that baby does not love herself, even though it implies neither that she does nor that she doesn't.

10. Since "All Greeks are human" goes over into logical notation as "$\forall x \, (Gx \to Hx)$," it is tempting to imagine that "Some Greeks are human" goes over as b instead of as a.

(a) $\exists x \, (Gx \,\&\, Hx)$ (b) $\exists x \, (Gx \to Hx)$

To see why a is the right translation, work out the trees for the inferences from a to b and b to a, and think about the counterexamples, i.e., cases in which b is true but a is false. (Draw circle diagrams.) Would you say that any of those are cases in which some G's are H's?

11. Alma is nearly (98 percent) certain that the Baron and the Count are the same man, and nearly (98 percent) certain that the Baron is mad. How nearly certain will she be that the *Count* is mad, if her credences obey the laws of probability?

12. Symbolize the argument in the box, and test its validity by the tree method. Is it sound? What are the truth values of its premises?

> This argument is unsound, for its conclusion is false, and no sound argument has a false conclusion.

5-5 MULTIPLE GENERALITY

"All the world loves a lover." That is another unexpectedly strong statement: it implies that if there is even one lover, then all love all. We construct a tree for that inference in Example 16. Meanwhile, let us see how to symbolize it, and how to draw some less remote conclusions from the same premise.

The premise means that everyone loves every lover, i.e., where the domain of the variables is all persons,

$\forall x$ (if x is a lover then everyone loves x)

Since being a lover is just a matter of loving someone, this comes to the same thing as

$\forall x$ (if x loves someone then everyone loves x)

In terms of the two-place relation *loves*, the antecedent says that $\exists y$ x loves y and the consequent says that $\forall y$ y loves x. Then the premise is

$\forall x$ (if $\exists y$ x loves y then $\forall y$ y loves x)

or, in full logical notation,

$\forall x \ (\exists y \ xLy \rightarrow \forall y \ yLx)$

And the conclusion says that if there is even one lover (if $\exists x$ x is a lover, i.e., if $\exists x \exists y$ x loves y) then all love all ($\forall x \forall y$ x loves y). Then here is the inference:

All the world loves a lover.	$\forall x \ (\exists y \ xLy \rightarrow \forall y \ yLx)$
If there is even one lover then all love all.	$\exists x \exists y \ xLy \rightarrow \forall x \forall y \ xLy$

That looks fairly nasty if you come upon it all at once, but if you build up to it a step at a time, it makes sense.

If you *should* come upon it all at once, you can decipher it by working backward. The conclusion is simple enough: a truth-functional compound of form $p \rightarrow q$. You can read that ("if p then q") as soon as you can read p ("$\exists x \exists y \ xLy$") and q ("$\forall x \forall y \ xLy$"), as you easily can, in various ways.

$\exists x \exists y \ xLy$: Some love some. Someone loves.

$\forall x \forall y \ xLy$: All love all.

Then the simplest readings of the conclusion seem to be these:

If some love some then all love all.

If someone loves then all love all.

If anyone loves then all love all.

(This last is not a mistake: in the antecedent of a conditional, "any" has the sense of "some," not of "all." Similarly, "If it's anywhere, Holmes will find it" and "Holmes, if anyone, can find it" make strong claims about Holmes's powers—claims that would become trivial if "any" were given the force of "all.")

As for the premise, it is a universal statement of form $\forall v\ (p[v] \rightarrow q[v])$ where v is "x" and the parts are readable:

$p[v]$	$\exists y\ xLy$	x loves someone	x loves	x is a lover
$q[v]$	$\forall y\ yLx$	all love x		all the world loves x

Then here it is, in simple Loglish:

For all x, if x is a lover then all love x.

In wooden English, this becomes

Everyone has the characteristic that if that
one is a lover then all love that one.

The rest is a matter of improving the prose:

Every lover is loved by everyone. All lovers are loved by all.

Changing to the active voice, we have these:

All love all lovers.   All the world loves a lover.

Now that we have translated that rather ambitious inference into and back out of logical notation, let us set it aside for a while, and work up to it by way of simpler inferences with the same rather complicated premise.

Example 13: Alma's Narcissism Inflames the Baron

All the world loves a
lover.
Alma loves herself.

The Baron loves Alma

1	$\forall x\ (\exists y\ xLy \rightarrow \forall y\ yLx)$	(prem)
2	aLa	(prem)
3	$-bLa$	(−concl)
4	$\checkmark(\exists y\ aLy \rightarrow \forall y\ yLa)$	(from 1)
5	$\checkmark-\exists y\ aLy \qquad \forall y\ yLa$	(from 4)
6	$\forall y\ -aLy \qquad\quad bLa$	(from 5)
7	$-aLa \qquad\qquad \times$	(from 6)
	$\times$	

Note that line 4 comes from line 1 by UI, with "x" as the variable **v**
and with the condition **p[v]** being "$(\exists y\ xLy \rightarrow \forall y\ yLx)$." Both occurrences of "x" there are replaced by "a" to get **p[n]** as in line 4,
i.e., "$(\exists y\ aLy \rightarrow \forall y\ yLa)$." Think of it in this way: the two occurrences or the variable "x" in the body of the premise are governed
by the quantifier "$\forall x$" out front. We can indicate this as in Figure
5-3, by drawing arrows from the quantifier to the two "x"s that it
governs. Now instantiation is a matter of removing the quantifier
and the variables, sliding "a"s in along the arrows to replace the two
"x"s that had been at their right-hand ends, and finally removing
the arrows.

It would be a mistake to imagine that since "a" was used as an
instance of "x" in the inference from line 1 to line 4, it cannot thereafter be used as an instance of "y," e.g., in the inference from line 6
(where the **p[v]** of UI is "−aLy") to line 7 (where the **p[n]** of UI is
"−aLa"). On the contrary, *all variables range over the same domain,*
so that as "a" is allowable as an instance of "x" in UI, it is equally
allowable as an instance of "y" in UI (see Figure 5-4).

Figure 5-3

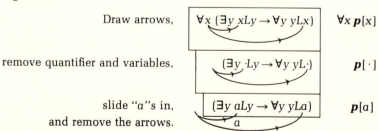

Draw arrows, $\forall x\ (\exists y\ xLy \rightarrow \forall y\ yLx)$ $\forall x\ p[x]$

remove quantifier and variables, $(\exists y\ \cdot Ly \rightarrow \forall y\ yL\cdot)$ $p[\cdot]$

slide "a"s in,
and remove the arrows. $(\exists y\ aLy \rightarrow \forall y\ yLa)$ $p[a]$

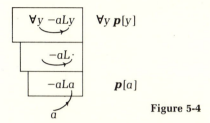

Figure 5-4

To underline the fact that all variables have the same domain, we rewrite "All the world loves a lover" as at the right below, and use it in that form as a premise in the next two examples. (In Example 13 it appeared as at the left, with "y"s in place of the two "z"s.)

$$\forall x\ (\exists y\ xLy \rightarrow \forall y\ yLx) \qquad \forall x\ (\exists y\ xLy \rightarrow \forall z\ zLx)$$

The two statements in logical notation are equivalent. In each, the purpose of the variables is *only* to indicate which quantifiers govern the four positions flanking the "L"s, as indicated by the links above. Indeed, the links alone give all needful information about such cross-indexing, as at the left in Figure 5-5. But to give that same information in a single line of type, we mark the two ends of each (invisible) link by occurrences of the same variable, taking care to do this in a way that makes it possible to reconstruct the original pattern by linking each variable next to an "L" with the first quantifier to the left of it that uses the same variable (Figure 5-5). Observe that the pattern of unlabeled links *is* recoverable from the unlinked labels by tracing left in the manner just described.

Figure 5-5 **(a) Unlabeled links. (b) Labeled links. (c) Unlinked labels.**

$\forall\ (\exists \cdot L \cdot \rightarrow \forall \cdot L \cdot)$	$\forall\ (\exists \cdot L \cdot \rightarrow \forall \cdot L \cdot)$	$\forall x\ (\exists y\ xLy \rightarrow \forall y\ yLx)$
(a)	(b)	(c)

Example 14: The Baron's Love Is Requited

All the world loves a lover.
The Baron loves Alma.
_____
Alma loves the Baron.

1	$\forall x\,(\exists y\,xLy \to \forall z\,zLx)$	(prem)
2	bLa	(prem)
3	$-aLb$	(−concl)
4	$\sqrt{}\,\exists y\,bLy \to \forall z\,zLb$	(from 1)

5	$-\exists y\,bLy$	$\forall z\,zLb$	(from 4)
6	$\forall y\,-bLy$	aLb	(from 5)
7	$-bLa$	$\times$	(from 6)
	$\times$		

Example 15: Alma Is Inflamed by Her Own Narcissism

All love all lovers.
Alma loves herself.
_____
Alma loves the Baron.

1	$\forall x\,(\exists y\,xLy \to \forall z\,zLx)$		(prem)
2	aLa		(prem)
3	$-aLb$		(−concl)
4	$\sqrt{}\,\exists y\,aLy \to \forall z\,zLa$		(from 1)
5	$\sqrt{}\,\exists y\,bLy \to \forall z\,zLb$		(from 1)
6	$\sqrt{}\,-\exists y\,aLy$	$\forall z\,zLa$	(from 4)
7	$\forall y\,-aLy$		(from 6)
8	$-aLa$		(from 7)
	$\times$		
9		$\sqrt{}\,-\exists y\,bLy\quad \forall z\,zLb$	(from 5)
10		$\forall y\,-bLy \quad aLb$	(from 9)
		$\times$	
11		$-bLa$	(from 10)
12		bLa	(from 6)
		$\times$	

Example 16: Amor Vincit Omnia

At last we construct a tree for the inference that we translated at the beginning of this section:

All the world loves a lover. $\forall x\,(\exists y\,xLy \to \forall y\,yLx)$
_____
If one loves one then all love all. $\exists x\exists y\,xLy \to \forall x\forall y\,xLy$

One might usefully abbreviate this tree by displaying only the crucial steps, perhaps as at the right in Figure 5-6, where the overall strategy is plain. In the full tree (at the left in Figure 5-6) we display all four of the instances of line 1 that we might want to use (lines 11 to 14) in order to see which of them we really need.

Figure 5-6   Tree for the inference from "All the world loves a lover" to "If one loves one then all love all."

1	(prem)
2	(−concl)
3	(from 2)
4	(from 2)
5	(from 3)
6	(from 5)
7	(from 4)
8	(from 7)
9	(from 8)
10	(from 9)
11	(from 1)
12	(from 1)
13	(from 1)
14	(from 1)
15	(from 14)
16	(from 15)
17	(from 11)
18	(from 17)
19	(from 18/16)

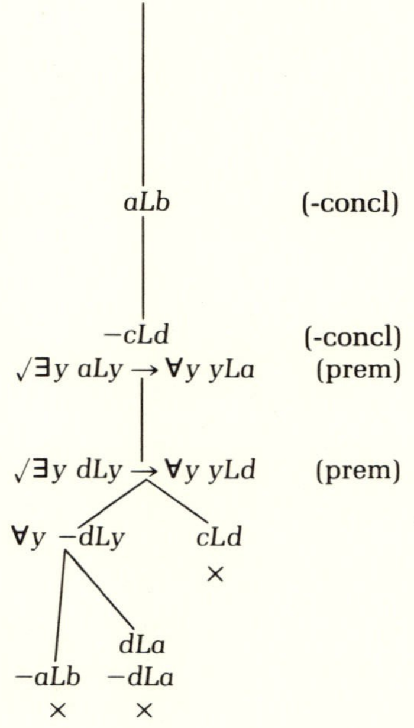

5-6   PROBLEMS

Use the tree method throughout.

1. Prove equivalent these two ways of saying that all the world loves a lover.
   (a) $\forall x \, (\exists y \, xLy \rightarrow \forall y \, yLx)$
   (b) $\forall x \forall y \forall z \, (xLy \rightarrow zLx)$

2. Test equivalence, and describe any counterexamples.
   (a) Someone is universally loved: $\exists x \forall y \, yLx$.
   (b) Everyone loves: $\forall x \exists y \, xLy$.

3. "B" means *is a brother of*. Domain: people. Prove equivalent the following two ways of saying that nobody is his or her own brother:
   (a) $\forall x \, -xBx$
   (b) $\forall x \forall y \, (xBy \rightarrow x \neq y)$

4. Test validity of the following inference.

At most one succeeded.	$\forall x \forall y \, ((Sx \& Sy) \rightarrow x = y))$
At least two tried.	$\exists x \exists y \, (Tx \& Ty \& x \neq y)$
At least one failed.	$\exists x (Tx \& -Sx)$

5. Test validity of the inference from "All circles are figures" to "All who draw circles draw figures." [Interpret "x draws circles" as "There is a circle that x draws": $\exists y \, (Cy \& xDy)$. Interpret "x draws figures" as $\exists y \, (Fy \& xDy)$.]

6. Test for validity the following modification of the circle-figure inference, in which the conclusion asserts that all who draw circles *thereby* draw figures:

   $$\frac{\forall x \, (Cx \rightarrow Fx)}{\forall x \forall y \, ((Cy \& xDy) \rightarrow (Fy \& xDy))}$$

7. Using "a" for *Alma* and "L" for *loves*, symbolize the following statements—building each out of its predecessor.
   (a) x loves y and y loves Alma.
   (b) x loves someone who loves Alma.
   (c) If x loves someone who loves Alma, then x does not love Alma.
   (d) None of Alma's lovers' lovers love her.
   Then test *satisfiability* of the set consisting of "Alma loves herself" and "None of Alma's lovers' lovers love her."

8. Does "No one knows everyone who knows him" imply "No one who knows himself is known by no one else"?

9. Symbolize and test for validity. (Domain: men. xOy: x is at least as old as y. Wx: x is wise. a: Methuselah.)

Any man at least as old as a wise man is wise.
Methuselah is at least as old as any man.
If there are any wise men, Methuselah is one.

10. Symbolize and test validity of this statement. "Not all acquaintance is mutual unless everybody who is acquainted with somebody is acquainted with somebody who is acquainted with somebody."

11. Symbolize and test validity of this (invalid) inference:

I'll be home before four.
_____

There's a time before four that I'll be home before.

(*Hx*: I'll be home at *x*. *xBy*: *x* is before *y*. *a*: four o'clock.)

12. Show that the foregoing inference becomes valid when we add the premise that *time is dense*: $\forall x \forall y (xBy \rightarrow \exists z (xBz \& zBy))$.

13. Symbolize and test validity of this argument. "Alma is an only child, for she loves no one, and only only children love only only children." (*a*: Alma. *xLy*: *x* loves *y*. *Ox*: *x* is an only child.)

14. Symbolize and show validity of this argument. "Brothers and sisters have I none, but that man's father is my father's son. Thus, I am that man's father." (*a*: *I* or *me*. *b*: that man. *xFy*: *x* is *y*'s father.)

5-7   FUNCTIONS

Adam begat Seth; Seth begat Enos; Enos begat Cainan. Here are two different ways of expressing these statements in logical notation:

Adam was the father of Seth:	aFb	$a = fb$
Seth was the father of Enos:	bFc	$b = fc$
Enos was the father of Cainan:	cFd	$c = fd$

In the first symbolization we represent the relation *was the father of* by a two-place predicate letter "F." In the second symbolization we use a different relation, *was* ("$=$"), together with a function symbol "f" for *the father of*. (We have not previously used function symbols in logical notation.) Here is the difference.

x was-the-father-of *y*	xFy
x was the-father-of *y*	$x = fy$

Names and variables are *terms,* and function symbols may be applied to terms to yield new terms. Thus, substituting equals for equals in the genealogy, we now have three new ways of designating Adam (*a*):

father of Seth	grandfather of Enos	great-grandfather of Cainan
fb	*ffc*	*fffd*

If the function symbol "*f*" is to produce a designator whenever it is applied to one, the function must be defined in such a way that there is always exactly one object *fx* corresponding to each object *x*. Then, according to Genesis, *the father of* will not do as an interpretation of "*f*," for if *x* is Adam (or Eve), there is no such object as *fx*. We might remedy this defect by arbitrarily deciding what values the function *f* is to assume, when applied to such arguments. Thus, we might define *f* as follows:

$$fx = \begin{cases} \text{the father of } x, \text{ if } x \text{ has a father} \\ x, \text{ if } x \text{ has no father} \end{cases}$$

Then since Adam had no father, we have

$$a = fa, \qquad a = ffa, \qquad \ldots$$

(These statements do *not* mean that Adam was his own father, his own grandfather, etc., for now "*f*" does not simply mean *the father of*.) Similarly, *the teacher of* is not an allowable interpretation of the function symbol "*f*," for some have no teacher, and some have more than one.

Our general requirements about the interpretation of any function symbol (say, "*f*") can be put as follows:

Existence: $\forall x \exists y \; y = fx$

Uniqueness: $\forall x \forall y \forall z \; ((y = fx \; \& \; z = fx) \rightarrow y = z)$

Both of these statements will be counted as valid by the tree test if we treat such terms as "*fa*," "*ffa*," etc., as if they were names, except that *where EI requires us to use a new name, the new item must be a simple name:* a single letter that has not been used anywhere in the path.

Example 17: Existence

1	$\sqrt{}\,-\forall x \exists y\; y = fx$	(−concl)
2	$\sqrt{}\,\exists x - \exists y\; y = fx$	(from 1)
3	$\sqrt{}\,-\exists y\; y = fa$	(from 2)
4	$\forall y\; y \neq fa$	(from 3)
5	$fa \neq fa$	(from 4)
	$\times$	

The tree shows that the statement "$\forall x \exists y\; y = fx$" is valid. To get line 3 from line 2 by EI, we put a new *name* ("a") for "x." But to get line 5 from line 4 by UI, we put an old term ("fa") for "y" to make the path close.

Example 18: Uniqueness

1	$\sqrt{}\,-\forall x \forall y \forall z\;((y = fx\ \&\ z = fx) \rightarrow y = z)$	
7	$\sqrt{}\,-((b = fa\ \&\ c = fa) \rightarrow b = c)$	
9	$b \neq c$	
10	$b = fa$	
11	$c = fa$	
12	$fa \neq c$	(from 9, 10)
13	$fa \neq fa$	(from 11, 12)
	$\times$	

Validity of the statement "$\forall x \forall y \forall z\;((y = fx\ \&\ z = fx) \rightarrow y = z)$" is demonstrated by closure of the 13-line tree of which the crucial seven lines are shown above. (Lines 2 to 7 use the rules for $-\forall V$ AND $\exists v$. Lines 10 and 11 come from the omitted line 8, which is their conjunction.) Note the end game: the two inferences in the last five lines.

We shall not insist on always writing function symbols before their arguments, as in "fx" above. Thus, if the domain of the variables is the set of all the nonnegative whole numbers, we shall use the accent " ′ " for the *successor* function, written after its argument: x' will be the successor of x, i.e., the next whole number after x. Similarly, we shall want to symbolize functions of two or more arguments, and although we shall sometimes use the so-called "functional notation" for this, e.g., "$s(x, y)$" for the sum of x and y, we shall often use the more familiar notation in which the function sign appears between the two arguments, with parentheses flanking the whole to preclude ambiguity: "$(x + y)$" for the sum of x and y, and "$((x + y) \cdot z)$" for the product of that with z.

Example 19: The System Q of Robinson Arithmetic

Here the extralogical notation consists of the accent "'" for the successor function, the name "o" of the number 0, and the two-place function symbols "+" and "·" for addition and multiplication. The domain of the variables is the set of all nonnegative whole numbers, i.e., in the notation of Q:

$$o, \qquad o', \qquad o'', \qquad \ldots$$

The axioms of Q are the seven statements shown in Figure 5-7. The first three are general truths about the successor function. Q1: Distinct numbers have distinct successors; Q2: zero is not a successor; Q3: everything else in the domain *is* a successor. Q4 and Q5 together serve to define + in terms of o and ', in the sense that any true statement of form $(t_1 + t_2) = t_3$ is deducible from them, where each of the t's is a term built out of "o" and, perhaps, accents. Thus, Figure 5-8 shows that the truth "$(o'' + o'') = o''''$" (i.e., 2 + 2 = 4) is deducible from Q4 and Q5. Similarly, Q6 and Q7 define *product* in terms of *zero, successor,* and *sum*.

Q1	$\forall x \forall y \ (x \neq y \rightarrow x' \neq y')$
Q2	$\forall x \ o \neq x'$
Q3	$\forall x \ (x \neq o \rightarrow \exists y \ x = y')$
Q4	$\forall x \ (x + o) = x$
Q5	$\forall x \forall y \ (x + y') = (x + y)'$
Q6	$\forall x \ (x \cdot o) = o$
Q7	$\forall x \forall y \ (x \cdot y') = ((x \cdot y) + x)$

Figure 5-7   Axioms of Q.

1	$\forall x \ (x + o) = x$	(Q4)
2	$\forall x \forall y \ (x + y') = (x + y)'$	(Q5)
3	$(o'' + o'') \neq o''''$	(−concl)
4	$(o'' + o) = o''$	(from 1)
5	$\forall y \ (o'' + y') = (o'' + y)'$	(from 2)
6	$(o'' + o') = (o'' + o)'$	(from 5)
7	$(o'' + o') = o'''$	(from 4,6)
8	$(o'' + o'') = (o'' + o')'$	(from 5)
9	$(o'' + o'') = o''''$	(from 7,8)
	×	

Figure 5-8

5-8 PROBLEMS

1. Test validity by the tree method.

   (a) $\dfrac{a = b}{fa = fb}$ (b) $\dfrac{fa = fb}{a = b}$ (c) $\dfrac{a = fb}{\dfrac{b = fc}{a = ffc}}$ (d) $\dfrac{}{\forall x \exists y \forall z \ (fx = z \leftrightarrow z = y)}$

   (Of course, validity of the "inference" d amounts to validity of the statement under the bar—a statement asserting the existence and uniqueness of fx, for every argument x.)

2. Test validity by the tree method.

   (a) $\dfrac{\forall x \forall y \ x = y}{\forall x \ fx = x}$ (b) $\dfrac{\forall x \ fa = x}{\forall x \ fx = a}$ (c) $\dfrac{\forall x \ gfx = x}{\forall x \forall y \ (fx = y \rightarrow gy = x)}$

3. Symbolize each of the following, using "f" as a function symbol for *the father of* and "g" as a function symbol for *the mother of*.

   (a) a is b's paternal grandmother.
   (b) a is b's grandmother.
   (c) a is a father.
   (d) a is a grandfather.
   (e) a and b are (full) siblings.
   (f) a and b are full or half siblings.

4. Interpret "f" and "g" as in problem 3, read "P" as is a *parent of*, and read "Mx" as x *is male*. Describe the relationship between a and b as concisely as you can in English, on each of the following assumptions.

   (a) $a \neq b$ & $fa = fb$ & $ga = gb$
   (b) $aPfb$
   (c) $a \neq b$ & $faPb$ & $gaPb$ & Ma
   (d) $fa = fb \leftrightarrow ga \neq gb$
   (e) Mb & $\exists x \ (xPa$ & $fb = fx$ & $gb = gx$ & $b = fa)$
   (f) $-Ma$ & $\exists x \ (xPa$ & $fbPx$ & $gbPx$ & $-bPa)$

5. *Incompleteness of Robinson arithmetic.* The system Q is strong on particulars but weak on generalities, e.g., although all the particular statements

   (a) $o \neq o', o' \neq o'', o'' \neq o''', \ldots$

   are provable in Q, the corresponding generalization

   (b) $\forall x \ x \neq x'$

   is not. Similarly, none of the generalizations

   (c) $\forall x \ (o + x) = x$ (d) $\forall x \forall y \forall z \ x + (y + z) = (x + y) + z$
   (e) $\forall x \forall y \ (x + y) = (y + x)$ (f) $\forall x \ (o \cdot x) = o$
   (g) $\forall y \forall x \ (x' \cdot y) = ((x \cdot y) + y)$ (h) $\forall x \forall y \ (x \cdot y) = (y \cdot x)$

   are deducible from $Q1$ to $Q7$, even though all their particular instances are. *Use the tree method to deduce the first two statements in a from $Q1$ and $Q2$. Then prove that none of b to h are deducible from $Q1$ to $Q7$ by verifying that in the following interpretation, $Q1$ to $Q7$ are all true but b to h are all false. Domain: the nonnegative whole numbers 0, 1, 2, . . .*

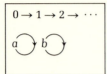

Figure 5-9 Problem 5.

together with two more distinct items, a and b. The function ′ can be diagrammed as in Figure 5-9, where arrows lead from members of the domain to their successors. The functions + and · have their usual values for their usual arguments. When one or both arguments are a or b, the values are given by the following tables, in which n is anything in the domain other than a and b, and n^* is anything in the domain other than 0, a, and b:

+	n	a	b
n		b	a
a	a	b	a
b	b	b	a

·	0	n^*	a	b
n			a	b
a	0	b	b	b
b	0	a	a	a

6. *Mathematical induction.* As shown in Figure 5-10, this is a "special" rule of inference, i.e., reliable in the usual interpretation of Q, but unreliable in others, e.g., in that of problem 5. The corresponding *tree* rule, "*MI*," has premises $p[o]$ and $-p[t]$ (t is any term), and a list of two conclusions, $p[n]$ and $-p[n']$ (n is a new name).* Using MI, closed trees can be constructed for the inferences from the axioms of Q to each of b to h in problem 5. Construct such trees for each of the following. (a) The inference from Q1 and Q2 to b in problem 5. (b) The inference form shown in Figure 5-10.

7. *The omega rule.* This rule (Figure 5-11) stipulates that any universal generalization follows from the infinite set of premises consisting of its instances for all nonnegative whole-number values of the universally generalized variable. It is cited here as an example of an *infinitary* rule: a rule that would allow infinite branches to close. (All our rules will be *finitary*, i.e., they use finite numbers of premises, and therefore all infinite branches will be open in trees that we shall consider.) *Problem:* Indicate the general appearance of a tree for the inference from Q1 and Q2 to "$\forall x \; x \neq x'$" using the omega rule but not the rule of mathematical induction. (Show the first four lines or so, and the last line.)

---

* The rule *MI* is adapted from Sue Toledo, *Tableau Systems*, Springer-Verlag, New York, 1975, p. 37 ("Complete Induction").

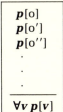

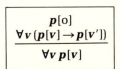

Figure 5-10
Problem 6.

Figure 5-11
Problem 7.

8. *The identity function.* We counted the one-place predicate symbol "=" as part of logical notation because it has no special subject matter, and because we can state its interpretation once and for all: if ***m*** and ***n*** are any terms, then

> The identity statement ***m*** = ***n*** is true or false depending on whether or not ***m*** and ***n*** denote the same item.

(Use of the particular symbol "=" for this purpose is merely conventional, but the fact that the purpose can be served in such a way is not.) Similarly we might classify as logical a one-place function symbol (say, "*i*") which has no special subject matter, and whose interpretation we can state once and for all: if ***n*** is any term, then

> The term ***in*** denotes the same item that ***n*** does.

Just as we introduced new rules of inference for the symbol "=" (one for identity, =, and one for diversity, ≠), so now we introduce a new rule of inference for "*i*":

> RULE FOR THE IDENTITY FUNCTION
>
> Erase occurrences of the $\sqrt{\boldsymbol{p}[\boldsymbol{in}]}$
>
> function symbol "*i*." $\boldsymbol{p}[\boldsymbol{n}]$

In first-order logic we have little occasion to use the notation "*i*," simply because it is redundant, as the rule testifies. *Problem:* Write out a four-line tree to show validity of the statement "∀x *i*x = x."

5-9   NOTES ON INTERPRETATION

Many-Sorted Logic

English provides different quantifiers for different sorts of domains, e.g., various universal quantifiers:

DOMAIN	Places	Times	People	Inanimate objects
QUANTIFIER	"Everywhere"	"Always"	"Everyone"	"Everything"

The corresponding variant of our logical notation would reserve different variables for different domains, e.g., "p" for people and "t" for times. In the following two examples, English statements are expressed in this two-sorted notation, and then reformulated in our usual single-sorted notation.

Example 20: "You Can Fool
Some of the People All of the Time"

Reading "F" as "can be fooled at," this statement can be interpreted in either of these ways, in the two-sorted notation:

    (a) $\exists p \forall t \; pFt$ There is someone who can always be fooled.

    (b) $\forall t \exists p \; pFt$ There is always someone who can be fooled.

In our usual single-sorted notation, all variables "x," "y," etc., range over the same domain, which includes people and times alike, in this example. Single-place predicates (say, "P" and "T") are needed to identify items in that domain as people or as times. In single-sorted notation, the first of these interpretations of the English statement might be written in either of these ways:

    (a) $\exists x \; (Px \; \& \; \forall y \; (Ty \rightarrow xFy))$ $\exists y \; (Py \; \& \; \forall x \; (Tx \rightarrow yFx))$

And, independently of which of these ways is chosen for the first interpretation, the second might be written in either of these ways:

    (b) $\forall x \; (Tx \rightarrow \exists y \; (Py \; \& \; yFx))$ $\forall y \; (Ty \rightarrow \exists x \; (Px \; \& \; xFy))$

The point is that in single-sorted logic, the same variable can play different roles in different statements, since the role is indicated explicitly in each case, e.g., by "Px" or by "Tx."

Example 21: "The Baron Was Alma's First Love"

In two-sorted notation we can express this thought by saying that there is a time t_1 at which Alma loved the Baron ($Labt_1$), and that if t_2 is a time at or before t_1 (if t_2At_1), she loved none but the Baron at t_2:

$$\exists t_1 (Labt_1 \ \& \ \forall t_2 (t_2At_1 \rightarrow \forall p (p \neq b \rightarrow -Lapt_2)))$$

The single-sorted version of this statement is more cluttered because of the need to explicitly identify variables as representing times or people, in ways appropriate to the quantifiers. Thus, if we use "x" and "y" for "t_1" and "t_2" and "z" for "p," as follows,

$$\exists x (Labx \ \& \ \forall y (yAx \rightarrow \forall z (z \neq b \rightarrow -Lazy))),$$

we must then put

"$\exists x (Tx \ \& \ \ldots)$" for "$\exists x \ldots$"

"$\forall y (Ty \rightarrow \ldots)$" for "$\forall y \ldots$"

"$\forall z (Pz \rightarrow \ldots)$" for "$\forall z \ldots$"

in order to get the correct single-sorted version

$$\exists x (Tx \ \& \ (Labx \ \& \ \forall y (Ty \rightarrow (yAx \rightarrow \forall z (Pz \rightarrow (z \neq b \rightarrow -Lazy))))))$$

of "The Baron was Alma's first love."

Categorical Statements

Statements in the notation of many-sorted logic often seem closer to their English counterparts than do their expansions into the single-sorted notation. Excellent examples of this are provided by the four forms of "categorical" (i.e., general) statements that were recognized in traditional logic (beginning with Aristotle, *De Interpretatione*, Chapter 7). These were regarded as subject-predicate statements, classified as *affirmative* or *negative* depending on whether the predicate is affirmed or denied of the subject, and as *universal* or *particular* (= existential) depending on whether the affirmation or denial concerns all things of which the subject terms is true, or only

A: ∀s Ps	E: ∀s −Ps
I: ∃s Ps	O: ∃s −Ps

A: ∀x (Sx → Px)	E: ∀x (Sx → −Px)
I: ∃x (Sx & Px)	O: ∃x (Sx & −Px)

(a) Many-sorted   (b) Single-sorted

Figure 5-12   The categorical forms in logical notation.

some. Traditionally, the four forms were denoted "*A*," "*E*," "*I*," and "*O*," as follows:

	AFFIRMATIVE	NEGATIVE
UNIVERSAL	*A*: All S are P	*E*: No S are P
PARTICULAR	*I*: Some S are P	*O*: Some S are not P

Their translations into many-sorted notation (with the variable "s" reserved for things of which the subject term "S" is true) and into single-sorted notation (where "x" ranges over S's and non-S's alike) are shown in Figure 5-12.

Existential Import

In single-sorted logic, the domain over which the variables range must not be empty. If it were, we would have no warrant for inferring "∃x Px" from "∀x Px," or for classifying "∃x x = x" as valid. (The nonemptiness assumption enters the tree method in clause 2 of the rule UI.)

Similarly in many-sorted logic, with (say) the variable "s" ranging over the S's, we might regard nonemptiness of the set of S's as a presupposition of normal use of the notation. In single-sorted notation that presupposition needs explicit statement:

∃x Sx   (*existential presupposition*)

The existential presupposition corresponds to a conversational implicature that arises in making statements of forms *A* and *E*, e.g.,

A	All my sloops are pretty.	∀x (Sx → Px)
E	None of my sloops are pretty.	∀x (Sx → −Px)

If I have no sloops, there is no serious point in my making either of these statements, for I can tell more by saying less: "$-\exists x\ Sx$." Thus, in making the *A* statement or in making the *E* statement, I normally give my hearers good reason to use the additional premise "$\exists x\ Sx$" in drawing inferences from it. But of course, if I deliberately make both statements *together*, I thereby cancel the existential presupposition that arises as a conversational implicature when I make just one of them. Thus, "All my sloops are pretty, and yet none of them are" is a ponderous joke—a roundabout way of saying that I have no sloops, pretty or not.

In the presence of the existential presupposition "$\exists x\ Sx$," used as an extra premise (or as an extra first line in every truth tree), the relations shown in the traditional square of opposition all hold. The terms "contrary" and "contradictory" are used in Figure 5-13 as they are colloquially: contraries cannot both be true (they are jointly unsatisfiable), and contradictories cannot both be true and also cannot both be false (they are jointly unsatisfiable, and so are their denials). But the traditional terms "subcontrary" and "subaltern" are now mere oddities. Subcontraries are statements that cannot both be false (their denials are jointly unsatisfiable), and in Figure 5-13, "subaltern" might be read as "implies": the claim is that *A* implies *I* and that *E* implies *O*. And these claims are correct *in the presence of the existential presupposition as an extra premise.*

Figure 5-13 Square of opposition.

Example 22: Subalternation

"All my sloops are pretty" (*A*) does not imply "Some of my sloops are pretty" (*I*), for I might have no sloops (in which case the premise would be misleading, but not false). But when "I have a sloop" is added as an extra premise, the resulting inference is valid.

5-10 DEFINITE DESCRIPTIONS

In English we can use names without implying or presupposing that they have actual bearers, e.g., we can say that Holmes used cocaine without implying that Holmes existed.* But whenever we classify something as a name in logical notation, we commit ourselves to the existence, in the domain of the variables, of something that the name refers to. Thus, if "a" is a name, then the statement "$\exists x \; x = a$" is valid, as the tree shows:

1	$\sqrt{} -\exists x \; x = a$	(−concl)
2	$\forall x \; x \neq a$	(from 1)
3	$a \neq a$	(from 2)
	$\times$	

In various examples we have reasoned about Holmes, Moriarty, and the rest—for the fun of it. Taken with obvious grains of salt, such reasoning serves well enough to illustrate the sober uses of logic where names have referents. But in literal talk, too, there may be doubt about the existence of one of the putative entities that are under discussion. Before 1930, someone might have speculated about the existence of a planet more remote than Neptune and provisionally assigned it the name "Pluto." The sentence "Pluto is less massive than the Earth" was not then known to be true or, indeed, to be a suitable vehicle for statement-making. That sentence makes reference to the one and only planet (if such there be) that is more remote than Neptune. If there *is* exactly one such planet, we want to be understood as saying that it is less massive than the Earth, and if there is not, we are prepared to admit that the presupposition was false, on the basis of which we proposed to use the word "Pluto."

---

* Or so it seems. But perhaps such cases are better described as ones in which we simply agree to speak falsely (on certain points), so that the assumption of existential import for names is *flouted*, but not suspended.

Then the needs of communication can be met by saying

There is exactly one planet more remote than Neptune,
and that planet is less massive than the Earth.

instead of the shorter but trickier

Pluto is less massive than the Earth.

The short sentence is tricky in that it conceals a possibly false assumption—an assumption that is made quite explicit in the longer version. If the variables range over the planets and we use the notation

a: Pluto

Px: x is more remote than Neptune

Qx: x is less massive than the Earth

then the long, explicit version can be written as

$$\exists x \, (Px \, \& \, \forall y \, (Py \to y = x) \, \& \, Qx) \tag{1}$$

in logical notation, where the short version is simply

Qa

It is the first two conjuncts in the long version that assert existence and uniqueness of a planet more remote than Neptune: following the existential quantifier, "Px" says that there is at least one, x, and "$\forall y \, (Py \to y = x)$" says that any other, say y, is in fact x itself (perhaps by another name). Finally, "Qx" says that this unique x is less massive than the Earth, and it says this only after the assumptions about x that are implicit in calling it "Pluto" have been made explicit.

Such, in outline, is Bertrand Russell's theory of descriptions.*
The rest is a matter of compression, notation, and jargon.

* "On Denoting," *Mind*, New Series **14**:479–493, 1905.

Compression

The statement that the one and only P has the property Q was represented in (1) above as the result of existentially quantifying a three-part conjunction. But the first two parts, which express existence and uniqueness of the P, can be combined and compressed: "Px & ∀y (Py → y = x)" comes to the same thing as "∀y (Py ↔ y = x)" because "Px" is equivalent to "∀y (y = x → Py)." Then we can rewrite (1) as

$$\exists x \ (\forall y \ (Py \leftrightarrow y = x) \ \& \ Qx) \tag{2}$$

or, changing variables and reversing the order, as

$$\exists y \ (Qy \ \& \ \forall x \ (Px \leftrightarrow x = y)) \tag{3}$$

("Something is Q, viz., the unique P.")

Notation

Russell used the following "iota" notation:

ɿx Px   the (unique) P

This "definite description" can appear in statements wherever names can, e.g., we can attribute the property Q to the P as follows:

Q ɿx Px   The (unique) P has the property Q.

But the expression "Q ɿx Px" is to be viewed as mere shorthand, to be replaced by a statement in the ordinary notation of first-order logic: (1) or (2) or (3) above. More generally, the defining property need not be expressed by a predicate letter; in place of "Px" we might have some such complex condition on x as "∀z (z ≠ x → xRz)," i.e., "x is more remote than any other planet." Nor need the property attributed to the unique such-and-such be expressed by a simple predicate letter "Q." In general, the defining property may be expressed by any condition $p[x]$ on x, and—using form (3) above— "Qy" can be replaced by any condition $q[y]$ on y, however complicated. Then Russell's formula for eliminating definite descriptions can be put as follows, in a generalization of (3):

$q[ɿx \ p[x]]$	$\exists y \ (q[y] \ \& \ \forall x \ (p[x] \leftrightarrow x = y))$
SHORTHAND	FULL STATEMENT

But of course, the variable in the shorthand version need not be "x," nor need the new variable in the full statement be "y."

Jargon: "Scope"

Where the condition **q** is complex, the iota notation is ambiguous. Russell's simple example is well known:

$-B \, ıx \, Fx$ The King of France is not bald.

Here the ambiguity of the iota notation corresponds to an ambiguity in the English, between these two:

$-\exists y \, (By \, \& \, \forall x \, (Fx \leftrightarrow x = y))$ It is false that the King of France is bald.

$\exists y \, (-By \, \& \, \forall x \, (Fx \leftrightarrow x = y))$ The King of France is nonbald.

In the first version **q** was the property B of baldness, while in the second it was the property $-B$ of nonbaldness. In Russell's jargon, the definite description "$ıx \, Fx$" has *narrow scope* in the first version and *wide scope* in the second. The scope is always the condition **q**, but where the (boldface) schematic symbols "**p**" and "**q**" are replaced by actual expressions in logical notation as in "$-B \, ıx \, Fx$," it need not be clear what **q** is to be (although the iota notation will always identify **p** unambiguously). There are various ways of complicating the iota notation so as to indicate the intended scope unambiguously,* but we shall simply suppose that where there is no presumption to the contrary, the intended scope is always the narrowest, so that, e.g., "$-B \, ıx \, Fx$" is interpreted as denying what "$B \, ıx \, Fx$" asserts.

$-Bıx \, Fx$	$-\exists y \, (By \, \& \, \forall x \, (Fx \leftrightarrow x = y))$	$\exists y \, (-By \, \& \, \forall x \, (Fx \leftrightarrow x = y))$
SHORT-HAND	NARROW-SCOPE READING	WIDE-SCOPE READING

* For Russell's way of doing this, see A. N. Whitehead and Bertrand Russell, *Principia Mathematica*, Cambridge University Press, 1910; 2d edition, 1925, vol. 1, p. 173.

Russell's theory of descriptions has been hailed as a paradigm of philosophical analysis. Its striking feature is that the term $ɿx\ \boldsymbol{p}[x]$ is eliminated from full sentences in which it appears without actually being defined—not, anyway, in the expected form

$$ɿx\ \boldsymbol{p}[x] = \ldots$$

(where the dots on the right are to be replaced by some expression in logical notation). Instead of such an explicit definition, Russell provided a "contextual definition" or "definition in use": he showed how to eliminate the definite description $ɿx\ \boldsymbol{p}[x]$ from any context $\boldsymbol{q}$ in which it might be found, but this elimination was no simple matter of substituting equals for equals. On the contrary, Russell analyzed (say) "The King of France is bald" as no simple subject-predicate statement but a far more complicated one, in which two different quantified variables occur. On Russell's theory, the deep structure of such statements is very different from what their surface grammar suggests.

5-11 PROBLEMS

1. *"Once a lady, always a lady."* This adage might be read in two ways. On the more plausible reading, "always" has the sense of "always thereafter," and the inference at the left is invalid.

Once a lady, always a lady.	$\forall p\ (\exists t\ pLt \rightarrow \forall t\ pLt)$
Alma's no lady.	$- aLn$
She never will be.	$\forall t\ (nAt \rightarrow -aLt)$

At the right, the adage is given a simpler, less plausible reading in two-sorted notation with "aLn" for "Alma is a lady now" and "A" as in Example 21.

(a) Use a suitable variant of the tree method to prove validity of the two-sorted inference at the right above.

(b) On the more plausible reading of the adage, transcribe the following inference into two-sorted notation, and prove it valid by the variant of the tree method used in (a).

Once a lady, always a lady.
Alma's no lady.

She never was.

(c) On the model of Example 21, transform into single-sorted notation the two-sorted inferences of (a) and (b), adding such additional premises as are needed in order to make the results valid.

2. *The square of opposition.* Which of the relations shown in Figure 5-13 are violated when the treatment of the categorical forms in Section 5-9 is modified in the following ways?

   (a) They are symbolized as in Figure 5-12b, but the existential presupposition "∃x Sx" is not used.

   (b) The existential presupposition is actually conjoined to the two universal forms, so that the symbolization is as follows:

   A: ∃x Sx & ∀x (Sx → Px) E: ∃x Sx & ∀x (Sx → −Px)

   I: ∃x (Sx & Px) O: ∃x (Sx & −Px)

3. *Plurality.*

   (a) In English, and in logical notation with Russell's iota operator, each of the four categorical forms has a conversational implicature stronger than the simple existential presupposition "∃x Sx":

   ∃x∃y (Sx & Sy & x ≠ y)

   Explain why.

   (b) In fact, "All my sloops are pretty" has an even stronger conversational implicature, which would be written as follows in logical notation:

   ∃x∃y∃z (Sx & Sy & Sz & x ≠ y & x ≠ z & y ≠ z)

   So have the other three categorical forms, in English. Explain.

4. By the tree method, prove equivalent the following four transcriptions of "Q ιx Px" into unabbreviated notation:

   (a) ∃x (Px & Qx) & ∀x∀y ((Px & Py) → x = y)

   (b) ∀x (Px → Qx) & ∃x∀y (Py ↔ y = x)

   (c) ∃x (Px & Qx & ∀y (Py → y = x))

   (d) ∃x (Qx & ∀y (Py ↔ y = x))

   Notice that you need only verify a cycle of four implications.

5. Prove that the wide- and narrow-scope readings of "−B ιx Fx" have the same truth value when there is exactly one F.

6. Eliminate the definite descriptions.

   (a) Alma loves her (unique) lover: aL ιx xLa

   (b) Scott is the author of *Waverley:* s = ιx Wx

   (c) Alma is fortunate if she loves her (unique) lover.

   (d) All are fortunate who love their (unique) lovers.

   (e) The author of *Ivanhoe* is the author of *Waverley.* (Use "ιz Iz" for "the author of *Ivanhoe.*")

7. "One of every two is *F*" is often used as an emphatic way of saying that half are *F*; but if either of the following inferences is valid, that usage cannot be strictly correct.

(a) At least one of every two people is female.

If someone is not female, then everybody else is.

(b) Exactly one of every two people is female.

There are fewer than three people.

Test both inferences for validity.

8. Translate into logical notation.
   (a) Some know all.
   (b) Some know all who know Alma.
   (c) Some know all who know them.
   (d) Some know all who know themselves.
   (e) Some who know themselves know Alma.
   (f) All who know Alma know themselves.
   (g) All who know all know some who know Alma.
   (h) Anyone who knows everyone Alma knows knows Alma.
   (i) No one who knows someone Alma knows knows all who know Alma.
   (j) All who know everyone Alma knows know some who know Alma.

UNDECIDABILITY

ith the full tree method for first-order logic before us, we now turn to questions of adequacy: *decidability* in this chapter, and *correctness* and *completeness* in Chapter 7.

It would be lovely if the tree method always gave the correct answers to questions of the form

Is this inference valid?

or (what comes to the same thing) of the form

Is this set of statements unsatisfiable?

Alas, it does not—not because it sometimes gives incorrect answers to such questions, but because in some cases it gives no answer at all. Thus, the tree method lacks the desirable property of decidability, and we are left with the large question (answered in this chapter) of whether there can be any improvement of or alternative to the tree method that does always give answers, and *correct* ones, to "yes/no" questions about first-order validity and satisfiability. The fact that the tree method sometimes gives no answer at all is readily seen from either of the following examples.

1	$\forall x \exists y\, xLy$	(prem)	a
2	$-aLa$	($-$concl)	
3	$\checkmark \exists y\, aLy$	(from 1)	
4	aLb	(from 3)	b
5	$\checkmark \exists y\, bLy$	(from 1)	
6	bLc	(from 5)	c
7	$\checkmark \exists y\, cLy$	(from 1)	
8	cLd	(from 7)	d

Figure 6-1 Tree for the inference from "$\forall x \exists y\, xLy$" to "$aLa$."

Example 1: An Unending Test of Validity

The inference from "Everyone loves" to "Alma loves herself" is invalid; and indeed, the tree never closes (Figure 6-1). But the tree is never finished, either, so that at no point does the test terminate with the news that the inference is invalid. Watching the tree grow, we can watch the growth of the counterexamples that are determined by the unending path: in the diagram beside the tree, each solid arrow goes from lover to beloved (according to the story told by the shortest statements in the path), and the broken arrow at the top indicates (see line 2) that Alma does not love herself. The story leaves out infinitely many details; e.g., Alma is the only character whose feeling about herself is specified, and we are not told how b feels about a, or about how a feels about c, etc. But any way of filling in all such details will be a counterexample: a case in which everyone loves somebody or other, but Alma does not love herself. Observe that nothing in the story forces us to take the characters other than Alma to be distinct from each other; the *story* is infinite, but for all we know, the names "c," "d," etc., might all be aliases for b. There are counterexamples (diagrammed in Figure 6-2) in which the domain consists of just Alma and the narcissistic Baron, whom she

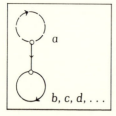

Figure 6-2 Counterexample for the inference in Figure 6-1.

loves. Perhaps he loves her; certainly, she does not love herself. To specify a particular one of these counterexamples, draw either a solid or a broken arrow from the lower circle to the upper one to get a complete case, with the Baron specified as definitely loving Alma (solid arrow) or definitely not doing so (broken arrow).

Example 2: An Unending Test of Satisfiability

Is the statement "$\forall x\, xLfx$" satisfiable? Yes; the infinite tree determines a class of interpretations in which the domain may be infinite (as suggested by the arrow graph at the right of Figure 6-3) or finite (as when that graph is converted into a closed loop by connecting the bottom arrow to the top node). Thus an overview of the unending tree test shows that the statement is satisfiable. Yet the tree test itself is inconclusive.

Clearly, the tree test does not always recognize invalid inferences or satisfiable sets of statements when it sees them. In that sense the tree method is inadequate, but in that sense, as we shall see, *every mechanical routine is inadequate:* there can be no adequate mechanical test for first-order invalidity or satisfiability. It follows that there can be no adequate mechanical routine for determining whether inferences have finite or infinite trees. Confronted with any particular inference whose tree is infinite, we may be able to recognize after some finite number of steps that the tree will never stop growing. But there is no uniform mechanical procedure for doing this; a procedure that works for some inferences must always fail for others, so that there is always place for human ingenuity in the matter of recognizing invalidity.

1	$\forall x\, xLfx$	(satisfiable?)
2	$aLfa$	(from 1)
3	$faLffa$	(from 1)
4	$ffaLfffa$	(from 1)
5	$fffaLffffa$	(from 1)
.		
.		
.		

Figure 6-3
Satisfiability of "$\forall x\, xLfx$."

We shall put the matter in this way: *the decision problem for first-order logic is unsolvable.* To put the same matter slightly differently: *there is no decision procedure for first-order validity.* The decision problem for first-order logic is the problem of devising a clerical routine which, applied by human being or machine to arbitrary inferences in the notation of first-order logic, eventually classifies them correctly as valid or invalid. The basis for the claim that this problem is unsolvable is a remarkable theorem proved in 1936 by Alonzo Church: that unsolvability of the decision problem follows from a certain hypothesis about computability.* That hypothesis is called "Church's *thesis.*" Thus, Church's *theorem* is the following assertion:

> If Church's thesis is true, the decision problem for first-order logic is unsolvable.

We shall prove this theorem below. But first we must state Church's thesis and explain its peculiar status as a hypothesis which there is good reason to accept but which is not susceptible of mathematical proof.

Toward this end we now introduce a very simple but remarkably powerful sort of computing machine, called an "abacus" or "register machine." These machines can be programmed to perform numerical computations, e.g., addition, multiplication, and others more complex. There is good reason to believe the following.

> **Church's thesis:** If a function is computable at all, it is computable by an abacus program.

Our strategy in proving Church's theorem will be to (1) define and illustrate the capabilities of register machines so as to make Church's *thesis* intelligible and plausible, then (2) define a particular function h and prove that no abacus program can compute it, and finally (3) show how the function h *would* be computable if there were a decision procedure for first-order validity. Then if register machines really are as powerful as Church's thesis says they are, the decision problem for first-order logic is unsolvable.

---

* Alonzo Church, "A Note on the *Entscheidungsproblem,*" *Journal of Sybolic Logic,* **1:**40–41, 1936; reprinted in Martin Davis, *The Undecidable,* Raven, Hewlett, N.Y., 1965.

6-1 HOW TO PROGRAM
A REGISTER MACHINE

As the name indicates, a register machine or abacus consists of a finite number of *registers,* each of which is capable of holding any finite number of objects called *counters.* By the *number* in a register at a particular time we shall simply mean the number of counters in the register at that time.

A *program* for such a machine is a set of instructions for putting single counters into registers and removing single counters from registers. If there are n registers, these are to be numbered from 1 to n, and the program will refer to registers by number. Among the simplest programs (Figure 6-4) is the one that adds 1 to the number in register r. The number in the circle (in the "node") indicates the register that is to be operated upon, and the plus sign following that number identifies the operation: *put a counter into register r.* Slightly more complicated is the program that subtracts 1 from the number in register r *if possible:* see Figure 6-5. If register r is empty, subtraction is not possible, and we leave the node on the arrow labeled "e" (for "empty"); but if there are any counters in the register, we can (and do) remove one, and we leave the node on the other, unlabeled arrow. If we bent the unlabeled arrow back to the "r-" node as in Figure 6-6, we would have a program for emptying register r, i.e., for setting the number in register r equal to 0. If the register is already empty, we go straight out on the "e" arrow, without doing anything. But if register r has one or more counters in it, we remove one of them and return on the other arrow to look once again and see whether the register is empty. If so, we go straight out on the "e" arrow, but if not we repeat the process—as many times as necessary to empty the register.

Figure 6-4   **Figure 6-5**   **Figure 6-6**

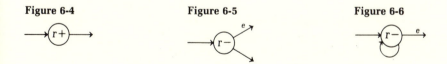

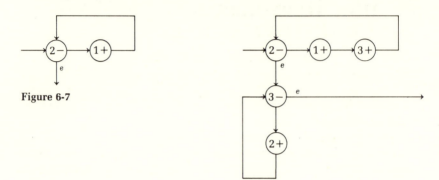

Figure 6-7

Figure 6-8

The two sorts of operations illustrated above suffice for all computations. Thus, the program of Figure 6-7 adds the number in register 2 to the number in register 1—emptying register 2 in the process, and leaving the sum in register 1. Here we remove a counter from register 2 and then add a counter to register 1, repeating the process until register 2 is empty. The effect is the same as if we had emptied register 2 into register 1 all at once by carrying box 2 over to box 1 and upending it. But the important point illustrated by Figure 6-7 is that the same effect can be had without resorting to any operations beyond the basic two: $r+$ and $r-$.

A somewhat more complicated program (Figure 6-8) lets us add the number in register 2 to the number in register 1 without emptying register 2. The upper subprogram empties register 2 into register 1 while duplicating the original contents of register 2 in register 3. Upon leaving that subprogram on the "e" arrow from the "2−" node, we go into another subprogram, which empties register 3 into register 2, thus restoring the latter's original contents *provided register 3 was empty initially.* (When the whole program ends, the number in register 2 will be the sum of the numbers originally in registers 2 and 3.) It is easy enough to modify this program so as to ensure that register 2 will have its original contents when the program ends even if register 3 is not empty initially: simply prefix a subprogram which empties register 3 before the main program begins, as in Figure 6-9. There the arrow running from the "3−"

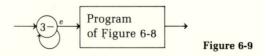

Figure 6-9

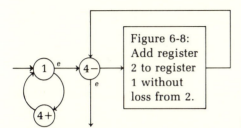

Figure 6-8:
Add register
2 to register
1 without
loss from 2.

Figure 6-10

node to the box is the arrow shown in Figure 6-8 as entering the "2−" node from the left, i.e., the *entry* arrow of the program of Figure 6-8. Similarly the arrow shown emerging from the box in Figure 6-9 is the exit arrow of the program of Figure 6-8: the "e" arrow from the "3−" node of Figure 6-8.

The adder of Figure 6-8 is easily modified to get the multiplier of Figure 6-10, in which the numbers to be multiplied are in registers 1 and 2, and registers 3 and 4 are empty initially. First, register 1 is emptied into register 4. Then the number in register 2 is added repeatedly to register 1, with each addition being preceded by the operation of taking a counter out of register 4. When register 4 is finally empty, the number in register 2 will have been added to register 1 a number of times equal to the number originally in register 1, and the multiplication is finished.

6-2 PROBLEMS

1. Initially there are x counters in register 1, y in register 2, and none in register 3 or 4. How long does it take to carry out the full program of Figure 6-10 if each $r+$ and $r-$ instruction takes 1 second?

2. Exponentiation is repeated cumulative multiplication: y^0 is 1, and for positive x, y^x is the product of x y's. Modify Figure 6-10 to produce a program for exponentiation. How long does the program take?

3. Superexponentiation is repeated cumulative exponentiation: sup $(x, 0) = 1$, sup $(x, 1) = x$, sup $(x, 2) = x^x$, sup $(x, 3) = x^{(x^x)}$, and in general sup $(x, y + 1) = x^{\text{sup}(x, y)}$. Modify your solution to problem 2 so as to get a program for superexponentiation.

6-3 CHURCH'S THESIS

For all their simplicity, the register machines we have been considering are capable of remarkable computational feats. We have seen how such familiar functions as the sum, the product, and the exponential can be computed by register machines. Further experience with programming these machines shows that they are capable of computing a very wide range of other functions—familiar and unfamiliar, simple and complex. Although abacus programs represent only one very special sort of clerical routine for computing functions whose arguments and values are natural numbers, it appears that every other sort of clerical routine can be transcribed for the abacus. Thus routines written in various programming languages and carried out on various commercially available high-speed electronic digital computers can be rewritten in the form illustrated above and carried out on abaci, to the same effect.

Church's thesis is the hypothesis that indeed no clerical routine that ever has been or can be invented is more powerful than the routines we have been examining, viz., abacus programs; it is the hypothesis that if a function is computable at all, it is computable by some abacus program. (We are speaking here of functions whose arguments and values are natural numbers.) This thesis is not susceptible of mathematical proof, for there is no limit to the variety of forms that clerical routines might assume, and thus no general, precise definition of the term "clerical routine" of the sort we would need in order to *prove* Church's thesis. In contrast, the notion of abacus program is very clear, and could be defined quite precisely. The same is true of every other particular sort of clerical routine, but the notion of *clerical routine in general* seems to defy precise definition.

But although Church's thesis cannot be proved, it might be refuted, *if it is false*. For if it is false, there will be some clerical routine which could in principle be specified quite precisely and which allows one to compute some definite function f that no abacus can compute. Since the term "abacus program" is precisely definable, we can hope to *prove* that no such program computes f.

Thus, Church's thesis is refutable if false, but stands so far unrefuted. Confidence in it is based on the fact that perverse human ingenuity has not managed to invent a clerical routine that cannot be transcribed for the abacus. Church's thesis may be false, but that possibility remains vague and speculative. At present the thesis is our only working hypothesis and so, lacking competition, commands credence. If, like newtonian dynamics, it is destined to be replaced by a deeper account, we are as yet in the position of lacking any notion of the shape that such an account might take.

6-4 UNSOLVABILITY OF THE HALTING PROBLEM

We now define a certain function h, and prove that no abacus program computes it.

The very definition of h refers to an enumeration $f_0, f_1, f_2, \ldots$ of all functions of one variable that are computable by register machines. We can think of that enumeration as having been derived from a prior enumeration $A_0, A_1, A_2, \ldots$ of all abacus programs where, to eliminate trivial complications, we require that if r distinct registers are named in the nodes of a program, these must be registers 1 through r. (Thus, the program $\rightarrow \widehat{2+} \rightarrow$ will not appear among the A's.) To derive the enumeration of functions from the enumeration of programs, think of the argument n as initially stored in register 1 and think of the value $f_m(n)$ as stored in register 1 when the program halts. Now to compute $f_m(n)$, identify the program A_m and set it to work with n in register 1 and all other registers empty. If the program ever halts, the value $f_m(n)$ will be the number in register 1 at that time; and if the program never halts, $f_m(n)$ is understood to be undefined.

Details of the enumeration of programs are unimportant, as long as it is a matter of routine to determine what program A_m is, for each $m = 0, 1, 2, \ldots$, and as long as all abacus programs appear in the list—all, that is, in which the registers referred to in the program's nodes form an unbroken sequence starting with 1. For the fun of it, we might let A_0 be the zero-node program $\rightarrow$, which computes the identity function $f_0(n) = n$. (This program halts immediately, so that whatever is in register 1 initially is there finally.)

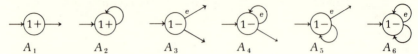

A_1 A_2 A_3 A_4 A_5 A_6

Figure 6-11   **The six one-node programs.**

Next might come the six one-node programs (Figure 6-11). Here are the functions that they compute:

$f_1(n) = n + 1$

$f_2(n)$ is undefined for all n

$f_3(n) = \begin{cases} 0 & \text{if } n = 0 \\ n - 1 & \text{if not} \end{cases}$

$f_4(n) = \begin{cases} \text{undefined} & \text{if } n = 0 \\ n - 1 & \text{if not} \end{cases}$

$f_5(n) = 0$

$f_6(n)$ is undefined for all n

And the list might continue with the two-node programs, the three-node programs, etc.—in which the registers referred to in the nodes form an unbroken block of numbers starting with 1. To specify the enumeration of A_m ($m = 1, 2, \ldots$) exactly, one would have to determine an order for the programs within each of these blocks, but as the thing can be done in various ways, and as one way is as good as another for our purposes, we shall not trouble to give the details.

We can now define the function h:

$$h(m, n) = \begin{cases} 0 & \text{if } f_m(n) \text{ is defined} \\ 1 & \text{if not} \end{cases}$$

The letter "h" is for "halt": $h(m, n)$ is 0 or 1 depending on whether program A_m does or does not eventually halt, once started with n in register 1 and all other registers empty. The *halting problem* is the problem of designing an abacus program that computes the function h. We now show that this problem is unsolvable.

What would it be, for the function h to be computable? It would mean that there exists an abacus program—call it "H"—that, started with m in register 1, n in register 2, and all other registers empty, eventually halts with $h(m, n)$ in register 1. Thus, the two arguments of the function h are stored in registers 1 and 2, and its value appears in register 1.

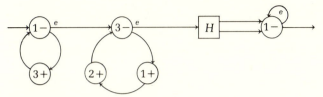

Figure 6-12

To show that there can be no such abacus program H, we now deduce a contradiction from the supposition that H exists.

If H exists, then so does the program depicted in Figure 6-12, where, for definiteness, the H program is represented as having two exit arrows. (The exact number is unimportant. Since $h(m, n)$ is never undefined, the H program must have at least one exit arrow.) If we start this program with some number in register 1 and all other registers empty, then the effect of the first five nodes is to reproduce that number in register 2 so that the H program starts with the same number in registers 1 and 2, and all other registers empty.

If H exists, the program of Figure 6-12 exists and computes some function f_m in our enumeration of all abacus-computable functions of one variable. Now consider the value (if any) that f_m assigns to m itself.

Case 1. $f_m(m)$ is defined, i.e., we eventually reach the exit arrow of Figure 6-12, after starting with m in register 1 and all other registers empty. But that can happen only if register 1 was *not* empty when we started down one of the exit arrows from the H subprogram, i.e., only if $h(m, m)$ is 1, not 0. But by definition of the function h, above, this means that $f_m(m)$ is not defined after all. Then case 1 cannot arise.

Case 2. $f_m(m)$ is undefined. Then we go round the "e" loop forever, at the end of Figure 6-12. But then, register 1 must have been empty when we emerged from the H subprogram, and thus $h(m, m)$ must be 0, not 1. But by definition of the function h, this means that $f_m(m)$ is defined, after all. Then case 2 cannot arise.

If the function h is abacus-computable, then the program H exists and either case 1 or case 2 must arise. But as we have just seen, neither case can arise. Conclusion: the function h is not abacus-computable. The halting problem for abacus programs is not abacus-solvable.

If Church's thesis is true, this shows that the halting problem for abacus programs is *absolutely* unsolvable: unsolvable not only by abacus programs, but by any clerical routine whatever.

Warning: Unsolvability of the halting problem does not mean that there are nonhalting programs that cannot be recognized as such or proved to be such. For any *particular* nonhalter we may be lucky or ingenious enough to recognize and prove that it never halts, once started with a specified number in register 1 and all other registers empty. Unsolvability of the halting problem means rather that there is no *general mechanical* routine for recognizing nonhalters: it is a matter in which luck or ingenuity cannot wholly be dispensed with.

6-5 TRANSLATING FLOW GRAPHS INTO LOGICAL NOTATION

Having proved the halting problem for abacus programs to be unsolvable, we can prove the decision problem for first-order logic to be unsolvable by *reducing* the halting problem to it, i.e., providing a routine method for converting any solution to the decision problem into a solution to the halting problem. As Church's thesis implies unsolvability of the latter, it must then imply unsolvability of the former problem as well.

The reduction will be a clerical routine applicable to any abacus program (say, A_m) and any natural number (say, n) to yield an inference in the notation of first-order logic together with three nonlogical symbols. In Section 6-7 we describe that routine and prove that the inference it yields is valid if and only if *the program A_m eventually halts, once started with the number n in register 1 and all other registers empty*, i.e., iff $f_m(n)$ is defined. Ability routinely to classify such inferences as valid or invalid would then confer ability routinely to classify programs as halters or nonhalters.

The inferences in question will be written in the notation of first-order logic (without "$=$") together with three nonlogical symbols: "o," "'," and "R." In the intended interpretation, the domain is the set of all natural numbers 0, 1, 2, . . . ; "o" is a name denoting the number 0; "'" is a one-place function symbol written *after* its argument and interpreted as $+1$ (so that "o'," "o''," . . . will denote the numbers 1, 2, . . .); and "R" is a many-place predicate letter, the intended interpretation of which will be explained directly.

If r distinct registers are named in the program's nodes, then "R" will be an $(r + 2)$-place predicate letter. We shall suppose that the registers named in the nodes are numbered 1 through r. If there are $N + 1$ arrows in the program, we shall number them $0, 1, \ldots, N$, using 0 for the entry arrow. We shall imagine that when a program is run on an abacus, it takes some definite time (perhaps, 1 second) to traverse an arrow and carry out the operation indicated in the node (if any) at the arrow's head. (If there is no node at the arrow's head, it is an exit arrow, and the operation is *halt*.) The beginnings of these successive periods will be numbered $0, 1, 2, \ldots$. Thus, at time 0 we begin to traverse the entry arrow, and before time 1 we carry out the operation indicated at the head of that arrow. Now in the intended interpretation, the predicate letter "R" is true of a sequence

$$t, i, c_1, \ldots, c_k, \ldots, c_r$$

of natural numbers if and only if the following is true:

At time t we start down arrow i with c_1 counters in register $1, \ldots, c_k$ in register $k, \ldots$, and c_r in register r.

Note: If the program halts before time t, then "R" is to be false of every $(r + 2)$-tuple that begins with t; and if i is not one of the numbers we have assigned to an arrow (if $i > N$), then "R" is to be false of every $(r + 2)$-tuple having i as its second member.

To see how this works, consider the program of Figure 6-13. Since there are four arrows, $N = 3$. Since two distinct registers are named in the nodes, $r = 2$, and "R" is a four-place predicate letter.

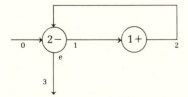

Figure 6-13

In the intended interpretation, register 1 has some number n of counters in it at time 0, and all other registers are empty at time 0. At later times, the contents of the registers are to be as specified by the program and the number n. Then in the interpretation determined by Figure 6-13 and the number $n = 2$, the statement

Rooo''o

will be a truth, describing the situation at time 0 (first argument of "R"), when we begin to traverse arrow 0 (second argument) with two counters in register 1 (third argument) and zero in register 2 (fourth argument). The statement

Ro'o'''o''o

will also be a truth, describing the situation at time 1, when we begin to traverse arrow 3 with 2 in register 1 and 0 in register 2. To avoid bedazzlement by long strings of accents, it will be wise to use abbreviations:

$\overline{1}, \overline{2}, \overline{3}, \ldots$

for

o', o'', o''', . . .

In general, "$\overline{n}$" will abbreviate a "o" followed by a string of n accents. To round things out, we interpret "$\overline{0}$" as another way of writing "o." Then we can write the foregoing descriptions of time 0 and time 1 as follows:

R$\overline{0}\,\overline{0}\,\overline{2}\,\overline{0}$ R$\overline{1}\,\overline{3}\,\overline{2}\,\overline{0}$

We can describe the program of Figure 6-13 in these terms, using a universally quantified conditional statement for each pair of arrows that respectively enter and leave the same node. The antecedent of the conditional will correspond to the arrow entering the node, the consequent will correspond to the arrow leaving the node, and certain details will be determined by the content of the node and by the presence or absence of the label "e" on the arrow leaving it. In Figure 6-13 there are five such pairs of arrows:

(0, 1), (0, 3), (1, 2), (2, 1), (2, 3)

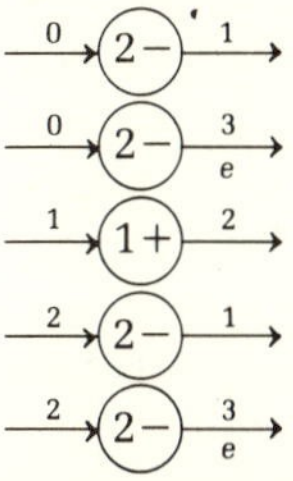

$\xrightarrow{0}\;(2-)\xrightarrow{\;1\;}$ $Rx\bar{0}yz' \to Rx'\bar{1}yz$ $(-)$

$\xrightarrow{0}\;(2-)\xrightarrow[e]{3}$ $Rx\bar{0}y\bar{0} \to Rx'\bar{3}y\bar{0}$ $(-e)$

$\xrightarrow{1}\;(1+)\xrightarrow{\;2\;}$ $Rx\bar{1}yz \to Rx'\bar{2}y'z$ $(+)$

$\xrightarrow{2}\;(2-)\xrightarrow{\;1\;}$ $Rx\bar{2}yz' \to Rx'\bar{1}yz$ $(-)$

$\xrightarrow{2}\;(2-)\xrightarrow[e]{3}$ $Rx\bar{2}y\bar{0} \to Rx'\bar{3}y\bar{0}$ $(-e)$

Figure 6-14 Statements describing the program graphed in Figure 6-13.

Of these, only the second will actually represent a path traversed when the program is run on a machine with two counters in register 1 and none in register 2 initially. But we write out the statements corresponding to all five pairs in order to give a complete description of the program.

Figure 6-14 shows the statements corresponding to the five pairs, with "$\bar{0}$," "$\bar{1}$," etc., instead of "o," "o'," etc., and with parentheses and universal quantifiers yet to be filled in.

There are three kinds of statements in Figure 6-14: one kind for a "+" node and two for a "−" node (depending on whether or not the outgoing arrow is labeled "e"). The kinds are indicated at the right. As they stand, the five formulas are abbreviations of statements. To get the full statement, enclose in parentheses and universally quantifty all variables; e.g., this is what the fifth formula abbreviates:

$$\forall x \forall y\, (Rxo''yo \to Rx'o'''yo)$$

We now consider the three types of statements, in turn.

The pair (1, 2) brackets a "+" node, and the corresponding statement (the third, above) says this, in the intended interpretation: *if at time x we start down arrow 1 with y counters in register 1 and z in register 2, then at time x + 1 we start down arrow 2 with y + 1 counters in register 1 and z in register 2.* In general, where there are r registers, where the incoming and outgoing arrows are labeled i and j, respectively, and where they bracket a node labeled "k+," the corresponding statement is the result of universally quantifying this conditional:

$\xrightarrow{i}\;(k+)\xrightarrow{\;j\;}$ $(Rx\bar{i}y_1 \ldots y_k \ldots y_r \to Rx'\bar{j}y_1 \ldots y_k' \ldots y_r)$

Here the y's can be any r variables distinct from each other and from "x," e.g., in the conditional for the pair (1, 2) above we used "y" and "z" instead of "y_1" and "y_2": the subscripts serve only to differentiate the variables. Note, too, that i, j, and k will be definite numbers, given by the labels on the arrows and in the node, e.g., in the conditional for the pair (1, 2) above, they are 1, 2, and 1, respectively. Thus, "$\bar{i}$," "$\bar{j}$," and "$\bar{k}$" are not variables; they stand for symbols "o" followed by the indicated numbers of accents.

The second and last of the five conditionals given in Figure 6-14 are of the $-e$ type. In the intended interpretation, the last of them says this: *if at time x we start down arrow 2 with y counters in register 1 and none in register 2, then at time x + 1 we start down arrow 3 with y counters in register 1 and none in register 2.* To put the same matter more succinctly: *if at time x we start down arrow 2 with register 2 empty, then at time x + 1 we start down arrow 3 without having changed the content of either register.* In general, the conditional corresponding to a $-e$ node is this:

$$\xrightarrow{i}\left(k-\right)\xrightarrow{j}_{e} \qquad (Rx\bar{i}y_1 \ldots o \ldots y_r \to Rx'\bar{j}y_1 \ldots o \ldots y_r)$$

Here the variable "y_k" appears neither in the antecedent nor in the consequent of the conditional. Instead, the symbol "o" appears as the $(k + 2)$nd argument of each of the "R"s.

Finally, the first and fourth of the five conditionals are of the $-$ type. In the intended interpretation, the first says this: *if at time x we start down arrow 0 with y counters in register 1 and z + 1 in register 2, then at time x + 1 we start down arrow 1 with y counters in register 1 and z in register 2.* The point is that if we have $z + 1$ counters in register 2 at some time, then register 2 cannot be empty at that time, for z can be no less than 0 (being a natural number), and therefore $z + 1$ must be at least 1. Then we shall leave the $-$ node on the arrow without the label "e," having removed a counter from register 2. In general, the conditional corresponding to a $-$ node is this:

$$\xrightarrow{i}\left(k-\right)\xrightarrow{j} \qquad (Rx\bar{i}y_1 \ldots y_k' \ldots y_r \to Rx'\bar{j}y_1 \ldots y_k \ldots y_r)$$

A small point: we have written the three sorts of conditionals as if k were neither 1 nor r and as if r were never 1 or 2, but we do not intend to exclude these cases. Thus if $k = 1$, the conditional just shown for $-$ nodes becomes this:

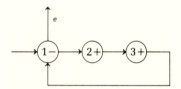

$$(Rx\bar{i}y_1' \ldots y_r \rightarrow Rx'\bar{j}y_1 \ldots y_r)$$

We no longer need display y_k separately, for y_k is y_1.

6-6 PROBLEMS

Assign numbers to arrows in each of the following programs, assigning the highest number to the exit arrow, and write out the quantified conditionals that describe the programs.

1. A_2

2. A_4

3. See Figure 6-15.

Figure 6-15   Problem 3.

6-7 REDUCTION OF THE HALTING PROBLEM TO THE DECISION PROBLEM

Having prepared the ground, we can now prove Church's theorem. Given any natural number n and any abacus program in which the numbers in the nodes are $1, \ldots, r$ and the arrows have been assigned numbers $0, \ldots, N$ (with 0 for the entry arrow), we specify the premises and the conclusion of *the associated inference* as follows.

The first premise is the description

$$R o o \bar{n} \ldots$$

of time 0, formed by writing a string of $r - 1$ symbols "o" in place of the three dots above. In the intended interpretation this says that *at time 0 we are starting down arrow 0 with n in register 1 and 0 in each other register.*

For each arrowhead and arrow tail that respectively enter and leave the same node, we write a premise, the details of which are determined as we have seen above by the numbers assigned to the arrows, the material in the node, and the presence or absence of a label "e" on the outgoing arrow. Recall that for pairs of arrows of the three sorts shown at the left below, we write as premises the universal generalizations of the conditionals shown at the right:

$$\rightarrow(k +)\xrightarrow{j} \qquad Rx\bar{i}y_1 \ldots y_k \ldots y_r \rightarrow Rx'\bar{j}y_1 \ldots y_k' \ldots y_r$$

$$\rightarrow(k -)\xrightarrow[e]{j} \qquad Rx\bar{i}y_1 \ldots o \ldots y_r \rightarrow Rx'jy_1 \ldots o \ldots y_r$$

$$\rightarrow(k -)\xrightarrow{j} \qquad Rxiy_1 \ldots y_k' \ldots y_r \rightarrow Rx'\bar{j}y_1 \ldots y_k \ldots y_r$$

There are no further premises.

For the conclusion, we want a statement that will or will not be deducible from these premises, depending on whether or not the program in question eventually halts, once it is started with n in register 1 and all other registers empty.

If the program has no exit arrows, then it cannot halt, and so a serviceable conclusion will be the denial

$$-R o o \bar{n} \ldots$$

of the first premise. (Actually, any statement false in the intended interpretation will do, for as the premises are all true in it, that interpretation would serve as a counterexample to the hypothesis that the inference is valid.)

If there is just one exit arrow—arrow number i, say—the conclusion is to be the statement

$$\exists x \exists y_1 \ldots \exists y_r R x \bar{i} y_1 \ldots y_r$$

that is true in the intended interpretation if and only if the program eventually halts, i.e., if and only if *there is a time x at which we start down arrow i* (the exit arrow), *with some numbers or other* $(y_1, \ldots, y_r)$ *in the several registers.*

And if there are two or more exit arrows—numbered $i, \ldots, j$, let us say—the conclusion is to be the disjunction

$$\exists x \exists y_1 \ldots \exists y_r R x \bar{i} y_1 \ldots y_r \vee \ldots \vee \exists x \exists y_1 \ldots \exists y_r R x \bar{j} y_1 \ldots y_r$$

This disjunction will be true in the intended interpretation if and only if the program eventually halts, i.e., if and only if *at some time we start down one of the* (exit) *arrows i, . . . , j.*

Having provided a clerical routine for writing out *the inference associated with* an arbitrary pair consisting of an abacus program (with numbered arrows) and a natural number, it only remains to prove the *reduction theorem*:

> The associated inference is valid iff the program halts.

Otherwise put, where f_m is the function that the program computes and n is the number initially in register 1: *the associated inference is valid iff* $f_m(n)$ *is defined.*

The proof is trivial in the "only if" direction, for by design, all premises of the associated inference are true in the intended interpretation, given that the program in question *is* started with n in register 1 and all other registers empty; and by design, the conclusion of that inference is true in the intended interpretation if and only if the program eventually halts. Thus, if the inference is valid (so that the conclusion is true in *any* interpretation in which all premises are true), the conclusion must be true in the intended interpretation. Thus, *if the associated inference is valid, the program eventually halts.*

In the "if" direction, the proof is easy, but not trivial. We first prove a lemma: for each $t = 0, 1, 2, \ldots$, the following holds:

> If the program has not halted before time t, the premises of the associated inference imply a "description of time t."

By a *description of time t* we mean a statement

$$R\bar{t}\bar{i}\bar{c}_1 \ldots \bar{c}_k \ldots \bar{c}_r$$

where t, i, and the c's are natural numbers. If a description of time t is implied by the premises of the associated inference, then it must be true in the intended interpretation, for all the premises are true in that interpretation. Note that if the program halts before time t, then there are no true descriptions of time t. ("True," unqualified, always means *true in the intended interpretation*.) Note, too, that if the program has not halted before time t, then there is one and only one true description of time t.

We prove the lemma by mathematical induction.

Basis. $t = 0$. Since the first premise is a description of time 0, the premises do imply such a description.

Induction step. The lemma is a conditional statement about all times $t = 0, 1, 2, \ldots$, i.e., a statement of form

$$-\boldsymbol{p}(\bar{t}) \to \boldsymbol{q}(\bar{t})$$

where $\boldsymbol{p}(\bar{t})$ means that the program has halted before time t and $\boldsymbol{q}(t)$ means that the premises of the associated inference imply a description of t. In these terms, what we need to prove for the induction step is

$$(-\boldsymbol{p}(\bar{t}) \to \boldsymbol{q}(\bar{t})) \to (-\boldsymbol{p}(\overline{t+1}) \to \boldsymbol{q}(\overline{t+1})) \tag{1}$$

It is an exercise in truth-functional logic to verify that (1) follows from

$$(\boldsymbol{q}(\bar{t}) \mathbin{\&} -\boldsymbol{p}(\overline{t+1})) \to \boldsymbol{q}(\overline{t+1}) \tag{2}$$

together with the obvious additional premise

$$\boldsymbol{p}(\bar{t}) \to \boldsymbol{p}(\overline{t+1}) \tag{3}$$

that if the program has halted before time t, then it has halted before time $t + 1$.

Then for the induction step it suffices to prove (2), i.e., in English:

> If the premises of the associated inference imply a description of time t and the program has not halted before time $t + 1$, then the premises of the associated inference imply a description of time $t + 1$.

There are three possible cases, depending on the values of i and c_k in the description

$$R\bar{t}\bar{i}\bar{c}_1 \ldots c_k \ldots \bar{c}_r$$

of time t.

      Case 1. i is the number of an arrow entering a node labeled "$k+$" from which arrow number j emerges. Then one of the premises of the associated inference is the universal generalization of

$$\overset{i}{\to}\!(k+)\!\overset{j}{\to} \qquad Rx\bar{i}y_1 \ldots y_k \ldots y_r \to Bx'\bar{j}y_1 \ldots y_k' \ldots y_r$$

whence we have

$$R\bar{t}\bar{i}\bar{c}_1 \ldots \bar{c}_k \ldots \bar{c}_r \to R\overline{t+1}\bar{j}\bar{c}_1 \ldots \overline{c_k+1} \ldots \bar{c}_r$$

by $r + 1$ steps of universal instantiation. In this conditional the antecedent is the description of time t implied by the premises of the associated inference. Therefore the consequent, which is a description of time $t + 1$, is also implied by those premises, and the induction step is proved in case 1.

Case 2. Arrow i enters a $k-$ node and $c_k = 0$. Suppose that the "e" arrow leaving the node is arrow number j. Then one of the premises of the associated inference is the universal generalization of

$$\xrightarrow{i} \boxed{k-} \xrightarrow[e]{j} \qquad Rx\bar{i}y_1 \ldots o \ldots y_r \to Rx\overline{'j}y_1 \ldots o \ldots y_r$$

whence we have

$$Rt\bar{i}\bar{c}_1 \ldots o \ldots \bar{c}_r \to R\overline{t+1}\bar{j}\bar{c}_1 \ldots o \ldots \bar{c}_r$$

by r steps of universal instantiation. Here again, the antecedent is the description of time t implied by the premises of the associated inference. Therefore the consequent, a description of time $t + 1$, is also implied by those premises, and the induction step is proved in case 2.

Case 3. Arrow i enters a $k-$ node and $c_k \neq o$ (so that $c_k = d + 1$ for some $d \geq 0$). Suppose that the arrow leaving that node *without* the label "e" is numbered j. Then one of the premises of the associated inference is the universal generalization of

$$\xrightarrow{i} \boxed{k-} \xrightarrow{j} \qquad Rx\bar{i}y_1 \ldots y'_k \ldots y_r \to Rx\overline{'j}y_1 \ldots y_k \ldots y_r$$

whence we have (by $r + 1$ applications of universal instantiation) a conditional of form

$$Rt\bar{i}\bar{c}_1 \ldots \bar{d}' \ldots \bar{c}_r \to R\overline{t+1}\bar{j}\bar{c}_1 \ldots \bar{d} \ldots \bar{c}_r$$

i.e., since $c_k = d + 1$, of form

$$Rt\bar{i}\bar{c}_1 \ldots \bar{c}_k \ldots \bar{c}_r \to R\overline{t+1}\bar{j}\bar{c}_1 \ldots \overline{c_k - 1} \ldots \bar{c}_r$$

where the antecedent is the description of time t that is implied by the premises of the associated inference, and so the consequent, a description of time $t + 1$, is also implied by those premises.

Then the induction step is proved in all three cases. That these are all the possible cases is guaranteed by the hypothesis (in the boxed statement of the induction step) that the program does not halt before time $t + 1$, from which we conclude that arrow number i, down which we start at time t, cannot be an exit arrow. It follows that arrow i must terminate in some node, and hence that one of cases 1, 2, 3 must hold.

This completes the induction step and, with it, the proof of the lemma:

> The premises of the inference associated with a program and a number imply a description of each time before which the program has not halted.

It only remains to get from that lemma to the "if" direction of the reduction theorem: *if the program halts, the associated inference is valid.*

Suppose, then, that the program halts—at time t, say, by starting down exit arrow i. Thus the program does not halt *before* time t, and the lemma assures us that the premises of the associated inference imply a (true) description

$$R\overline{tic}_1 \ldots \overline{c}_r$$

of time t. From this, by $r + 1$ steps of existential generalization, we infer a statement

$$\exists x \exists y_1 \ldots \exists y_r \, Rx\overline{i}y_1 \ldots y_r$$

which is either the conclusion of the associated inference (if the program has just one exit arrow) or a disjunct of that conclusion (if there are two or more exit arrows). In either case we can infer the conclusion of the associated inference, which is thus implied by its premises. The case in which the conclusion of the associated inference is the denial of its first premise cannot arise if the program halts, for to halt, it must have an exit arrow. Then if the program eventually halts, the associated inference is valid.

Then the reduction is genuine: the halters are precisely the programs whose associated inferences are valid. It follows that we could parlay any solution to the decision problem for quantificational logic into a solution of the halting problem for abacus programs, which we know to be unsolvable if Church's thesis is true. We have thus proved Church's theorem on the undecidability of first-order logic.

6-8   FOCUSING THE UNDECIDABILITY RESULT

We have proved unsolvable the general decision problem for first-order validity. We did that by reducing the halting problem for abacus programs to the decision problem for first-order validity of a certain special class of inferences, as follows. In Section 6-5 we described a clerical routine, applicable to the graphs of abacus programs, for obtaining associated inferences in the notation of first-order logic, and in Section 6-7 we proved that the associated inference is valid or invalid depending on whether or not the program is a halter. Then if the decision problem for first-order validity of associated inferences were solvable, so would be the halting problem for abacus programs, which we proved unsolvable in Section 6-4. Unsolvability of the general decision problem was merely a corollary of the unsolvability of the special decision problem for associated inferences.

What are the salient features of the special class of ("associated") inferences whose decision problem for first-order validity we have proved to be unsolvable? The answer is clearly suggested by the simplest examples. In considering these examples it becomes clear that we do best to ask, not about the inferences themselves, but about the corresponding sets of statements (essentially, the premises and denial of the conclusion) whose satisfiability or unsatisfiability comes to the same thing as invalidity or validity of the inferences.

Example 3: Associated Inferences for A_2 and A_3

These inferences are shown in Figure 6-16. Validity of these inferences comes to the same thing as unsatisfiability of the sets of statements shown in Figure 6-17a and b. As these examples testify, the inferences whose decision problem for truth-functional validity we have proved unsolvable have the following salient features.

Figure 6-16

$$A_2: \quad \xrightarrow{0} \text{\Large(} 1+ \text{\Large)}^1$$

$Rooo$
$\forall x \forall y\ (Rxoy \rightarrow Rx'o'y')$
$\forall x \forall y\ (Rxo'y \rightarrow Rx'o'y')$
$-Rooo$

(a)

$$A_3: \quad \xrightarrow{0} \text{\Large(} 1- \text{\Large)} \begin{smallmatrix} e \\ \nearrow 1 \\ \searrow 2 \end{smallmatrix}$$

$Rooo$
$\forall x\ (Rxoo \rightarrow Rx'o'o)$
$\forall x \forall y\ (Rxoy' \rightarrow Rx'o''y)$
$\exists x \exists y\ Rxo'y \lor \exists x \exists y\ Rxo''y$

(b)

Rooo
$\forall x \forall y \, (Rxoy \rightarrow Rx'o'y')$
$\forall x \forall y \, (Rxo'y \rightarrow Rx'o'y')$

Here I have omitted the denial "$- -Rooo$" of the conclusion, as it is equivalent to the first statement in the list.

(a)

Rooo
$\forall x \, (Rxoo \rightarrow Rx'o'o)$
$\forall x \forall y \, (Rxoy' \rightarrow Rx'o''y)$
$\forall x \forall y \, -Rxo'y$
$\forall x \forall y \, -Rxo''y$

Here I have replaced the denial of the disjunctive conclusion by a couple of statements that are equivalent to the denials of the disjuncts.

(b)

Figure 6-17

(1) The number of premises is finite. (2) Each premise is an "$\forall$ statement," i.e., *if it contains any quantifiers, they are all universal and come together in a block at the extreme left.* (3) The denial of the conclusion either is an $\forall$ statement or is equivalent to the conjunction of finitely many $\forall$ statements. (4) The sign of identity "$=$" does not occur in any of the premises or in the conclusion. (5) The function symbol "$'$" does occur. But apparently we can put matters more succinctly by speaking of the corresponding decision problem for satisfiability of sets of statements, in which the conjunctions mentioned in (3) can be replaced by the finite lists of their components as in Example 3 and lumped together with the premises. In these terms, we have proved the following.

> Unsolvable: The decision problem for first-order satisfiability of finite sets of $\forall$ statements in which the sign of identity does not occur (but in which function symbols may occur).

In view of this fact, it is not surprising that in Example 2, the tree method failed to classify as satisfiable the finite set consisting of the $\forall$ statement "$\forall x \, xLfx$" alone. But note well: the claim is not that such sets cannot be recognized as satisfiable when they are, e.g., it is obvious that the statement that the tree test fails to classify in Example 2 is in fact satisfiable. The claim is rather that although satisfiability of finite sets of $\forall$ statements may be recognizable in each case, there is no uniform clerical routine for doing it; we cannot altogether dispense with luck and ingenuity in doing those jobs.

By way of contrast with the foregoing undecidability result, notice that if (as we show in Chapter 7) the tree test is *reliable* in the sense that when it does classify a set as satisfiable or as unsatisfiable that classification is correct, then the following problem is solvable.

> Solvable by the tree method: The decision problem for first-order satisfiability of finite sets of ∀ statements in which no function symbols occur (but in which the sign of identity may occur).

Proof. (It may be helpful to have an example in view, e.g., the set consisting of the statements "Everybody loves baby" and "Baby loves nobody but me," which is shown to be satisfiable by the tree test, as in Figure 6-18. There I have truncated the tree by omitting numerous lines that are obtainable from line 7 and others by means of the rule for identity, but which do not contribute further to the description of the interpretation, i.e., a domain of one person, who loves himself or herself.) So much for the example. In general, as there are no existential quantifiers, the only names that ever appear in the tree are the finite number of them that appear initially (unless there are none initially but there *are* universal quantifiers, in which case the rule for UI requires us to introduce a single name). Then only a finite number of distinct names will ever appear in the tree, and so after a finite number of applications of UI and the rules for identity, the only rules of inference that remain to be applied will be those for the truth-functional connectives. But as we saw in Section 2-4 (decidability of the tree test for truth-functional satisfiability), the process of applying those rules must terminate after some finite number of steps. At that point we shall be extruded from the program through one of the STOP arrows, with a classification of the

Figure 6-18   A test for satisfiability.

1	$\forall x\ xLb$	
2	$\forall x\ (bLx \to x = a)$	
3	aLb	(from 1)
4	bLb	(from 1)
5	$\sqrt{}bLa \to a = a$	(from 2)
6	$\sqrt{}bLb \to b = a$	(from 2)
7	$-bLb \qquad b = a$	(from 6)
	$\times$	
8	$-bLa \qquad a = a$	(from 5)
9	$-bLb$	(from 7, 8)
	$\times$	

initial set of ∀ statements as *satisfiable* or as *unsatisfiable*. The correctness of that classification will be demonstrated in the following chapter.

In conclusion, let us note that we could have reduced the halting problem to the decision problem for a somewhat different class of inferences, thus proving the following.

> Unsolvable: The decision problem for first-order satisfiability of finite sets of statements in which no function symbols occur (but in which the sign of identity may occur).

(Of course, in the interesting cases, not all members of the set will be ∀ statements.) Instead of proving this claim systematically, we shall illustrate how the reduction goes in the case of A_3 in Example 3 above. It will be obvious from that how the reduction would go in general. The main difference is that we now make the two-place predicate symbol "S" (for the successor relation, *is immediately succeeded by*) do the work of the function symbol " ' " followed by the sign of identity "=." Thus we write "xSy" instead of "x' = y," just as if "S" stood for the pair " '=." Where there are more accents, we use extra variables, e.g., we write "∀y (xSy → ySz)" instead of "x'' = z"; see Figure 6-19. (Note: We could write "∃y (xSy & ySz)" to the same effect.) And in order to ensure that the successor relation assigns one and only one successor to each number, we add the following two statements as additional premises, in the inference associated with each abacus program.

∀x∃y xSy   (*existence of successors*)

∀x∀y∀z ((xSy & xSz) → y = z)   (*uniqueness of successors*)

It then turns out that the proof in Section 6-7 can easily be modified to show that this new sort of associated inference is valid or not depending on whether or not the program is a halter. (But we shall not carry out that modification here.) Conclusion: If the decision problem for first-order validity of these inferences were solvable, so would be the (unsolvable) halting problem for abacus programs.

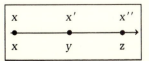

Figure 6-19

Example 4: The New-Style Associated Inference for A_3

It comes to the same thing, and is clearer, to display the set of statements whose joint satisfiability is tantamount to invalidity of the associated inference. These are listed in Figure 6-20a. Corresponding members of the set of statements in Example 3 above appear in Figure 6-20b.

Notice that *except for the first premise* (existence of successors), all statements in this new set are of the ∀ form; if the first premise were deleted, the tree test for satisfiability of this set would terminate after some finite number of steps. And that will be true for all new-style associated inferences: the class of all such inferences misses decidability only because of the presence in each of them of the insidious premise "$\forall x \exists y\ xSy$," which generates no end of new names.

Figure 6-20

$\forall x \exists y\ xSy$	(existence)
$\forall x \forall y \forall z\ ((xSy\ \&\ xSz) \to y = z)$	(uniqueness)
$Rooo$	
$\forall x \forall y \forall z\ ((xSy\ \&\ oSz\ \&\ Rxoo) \to Ryzo)$	
$\forall x \forall y \forall u \forall v \forall w \forall z\ ((ySu\ \&\ xSv\ \&\ oSw\ \&\ wSz\ \&\ Rxou) \to Rvzy)$	
$\forall x \forall y \forall z\ (oSz \to -Rxzy)$	
$\forall x \forall y \forall z \forall w\ ((oSz\ \&\ zSw) \to -Rxwy)$	

(a) New

$Rooo$
$\forall x\ (Rxoo \to Rx'o'o)$
$\forall x \forall y\ (Rxoy' \to Rx'o''y)$
$\forall x \forall y\ -Rxo'y$
$\forall x \forall y\ -Rxo''y$

(b) Old

n nodes

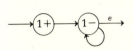

Figure 6-21 Problem 1.

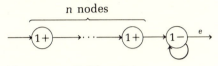

Figure 6-22 Problem 1(a).

6-9 PROBLEMS

1. *The busy beaver problem.* Define r(n) as the running time of the longest-running n-node programs that eventually halt when started with all registers empty. Here, *running time = number of passages through nodes,* e.g., r(0) = 0, r(1) = 1 (Figure 6-11), and r(2) = 3 (see Figure 6-21).

   (a) What is the running time of the program shown in Figure 6-22? Bearing in mind that this may not be the longest-running n + 1-node program, what can we conclude about r(n + 1)?

   (b) On the basis of Figure 6-23, what can we conclude about the relationship between r(n) and r(n + 1)? Explain why it follows that n > m if r(n) > r(m).

   (c) See Figure 6-24. If r is computable (say, by a k-node program R that does not use register 2), then we may conclude that r(n + k + 2) ≥ r(r(n)). Explain.

   (d) Prove unsolvable the ("busy beaver") problem of designing a program R that computes r. (Show that if that problem were solvable, k would be bigger than any positive integer.)

2. Using Church's thesis, explain how the busy beaver problem would be solvable if the halting problem were. (This provides a proof of the unsolvability of the halting problem independent of the one given in Section 6-4.)

3. *A decidable class of inferences.* A *prenex* statement is one in which all quantifiers (if any) appear in a single block at the extreme left, e.g., "∀x∀y∃z (yLz → xLy)" is prenex, but "∀x∃y (∃z yLz → xLy)" is not. An

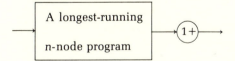

Figure 6-23 Problem 1(b).

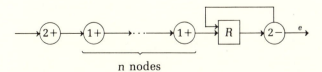

n nodes

Figure 6-24
Problem 1(c).

∃∀ statement is a prenex statement in which all existential quantifiers (if any) appear in a block to the left of any universal quantifiers, and an ∀∃ statement is a prenex statement in which all universal quantifiers (if any) appear in a block to the left of any existential quantifiers. Thus "∀x∀y∃z $(yLz \rightarrow xLy)$" is ∀∃; and ∀ statements are both ∀∃ and ∃∀. *Problem:* Assuming that the tree method is reliable (as proved in Chapter 7), prove the following.

> Solvable by the tree method: The decision problem for first-order validity of inferences with finitely many premises, all of which are ∃∀ statements in which no function symbols occur, and with conclusions that are ∀∃ statements in which no function symbols occur.

4. On the model of Example 4, write out new-style associated inferences (or, rather, the corresponding sets of statements) for the programs of Section 6-6.

5. Show by the tree method that in the presence of the two premises "∀x∃y xSy" (*existence*) and "∀x∀y∀z $((xSy \ \& \ xSz) \rightarrow y = z)$" (*uniqueness*), each of the following implies the other.

$$\forall x \ (aSx \rightarrow xSb) \qquad \exists x \ (aSx \ \& \ xSb)$$

6-10   HISTORICAL NOTE

The reduction in Sections 6-5 and 6-7 of the abacus halting problem to the decision problem for first-order logic was devised by George Boolos in 1974.* The result is a dramatic simplification of Alan Turing's (1936–1937) proof of what is here called "Church's theorem." Church's (1936) form of Church's thesis claimed universality not for abacus programs but for a clerical routine called "lambda-conversion." Versions of the thesis claiming universality for various sorts of machines or machine programs have been floated by Turing, Emil Post (1936), and others. Numerous other versions have been floated, claiming universality for a variety of clerical routines, e.g., by S. C. Kleene (1936), Post (1944), and A. A. Markov (1954). All known versions of Church's thesis have been proved equivalent, i.e., it has been proved that exactly the same functions are computable by each sort of machine or routine for which universality is claimed in the various versions of the thesis. This circum-

---

* Unpublished. The works cited in this section are listed in the References; see page 189.

stance has convinced those learned in the matter that computability is an *absolute* concept, i.e., that the various versions of the thesis are all true. The machines for whose programs universality is asserted in our version of Church's thesis combine the virtues of simplicity with similarity to existing computing machines. Abacus programs were introduced by Z. A. Melzak (1961) and given the form used here by Joachim Lambek (1962). Martin Davis (1965) has made a useful collection of the early papers on uncomputability. For proofs of the equivalence of several sorts of routines, see Martin Davis (1958), Elliot Mendelson (1979), and Boolos and Jeffrey (1980), among others. B. A. Trakhtenbrot (1963) presents a brief, readable introduction to computability and its limits, and Turing's popular article (1954) is a gem. Problem 1 in Section 6-9 is a minor variant of Tibor Rado's busy beaver problem (1962). The charm of the function r is that it refers directly to intrinsic characteristics of abacus programs, without the mediation of such arbitrary enumerations as were required in the definition of the *halting* function h. For overviews of the current state of the decision problem for various classes of statements, see Dreben and Goldfarb (1979) and Harry R Lewis (1979).

COMPLETENESS AND INCOMPLETENESS

We now prove that the tree method is a reliable clerical routine for recognizing first-order validity, but that for second-order logic there can be no such routine. Thus, we prove Kurt Gödel's completeness theorem for first-order logic, and his incompleteness theorem for higher-order logic. (Completeness of first-order logic is compatible with undecidability, as the latter property arises from lack of a general clerical routine that reliably recognizes first-order *invalidity;* but for second-order logic there can be no such general routine for validity or for invalidity.)

7-1   HIGHER-ORDER LOGIC

The term "higher-order logic" refers to a hierarchy that has a bottom, 0th level, but has no top; see Figure 7-1. The items at level 0 are simply the items in the domain over which the variables "x," "y," etc., range in first-order logic: people (as in the story of Alma), numbers (as in Robinson arithmetic), or whatever. The term "individuals" is meant to be a neutral designation for whatever items may have been assigned to the ground level—even if these are items like states or properties that would not ordinarily be identified as individuals. It is with that understanding that we speak of "x" and "y" as *individual variables* and of "a" and "b" as *individual constants.* The only predicate symbols we have encountered so far have been predicate constants of level 1, e.g., the predicate letter "L" (*loves*) in the story

Level 3:	Predicates of items at levels 0, 1, 2
Level 2:	Predicates of items at levels 0, 1
Level 1:	Predicates of items at level 0
Level 0:	"Individuals"

Figure 7-1 Hierarchy of logical types.

of Alma and the symbol "=" for the relation of identity between individuals. But we can easily define second-level predicate constants, e.g., for the second-level properties that first-level properties have when they apply to exactly n things ($n = 0, 1, 2, \ldots$).

Example 1: Nonnegative Whole Numbers as Properties

The cardinal numbers $0, 1, 2, \ldots$ were analyzed by Gottlob Frege* as properties of properties, e.g., 0 is the property that the property A has in case it applies to nothing:

$$\forall A \ (0A \leftrightarrow -\exists x \ Ax)$$

Here "A" is used as a first-level variable. (This is just where second-order logic differs from first-order logic, i.e., in permitting generalization of first-level symbols.) Just as "$0A$" means that there are no A's, so "$1A$" means that there is exactly one A, i.e., at least one, $\exists x \ Ax$, and at most one, $\forall x \forall y \ ((Ax \ \& \ Ay) \rightarrow x = y)$:

$$\forall A \ (1A \leftrightarrow (\exists x \ Ax \ \& \ \forall x \forall y \ ((Ax \ \& \ Ay) \rightarrow x = y)))$$

Similarly, $2A$ will be defined by the conjunction of these:

$$\exists x \exists y \ (Ax \ \& \ Ay \ \& \ x \neq y) \qquad \text{(at least 2)}$$

$$\forall x \forall y \forall z \ ((Ax \ \& \ Ay \ \& \ Az) \rightarrow (x = y \lor x = z \lor y = z)) \quad \text{(at most 2)}$$

---

* *Grundgesetze der Arithmetik*, vol. 1, Jena, 1893. See translation and commentary by Montgomery Furth, *The Basic Laws of Arithmetic*, University of California Press, Berkeley and Los Angeles, 1964.

And so on. These definitions can be made more compact by running the "at least n" and "at most n" clauses together, either like this:

$$1A \leftrightarrow \exists x \, (Ax \,\&\, \forall y \, (Ay \rightarrow y = x))$$

$$2A \leftrightarrow \exists x \exists y \, (Ax \,\&\, Ay \,\&\, x \neq y \,\&\, \forall z \, (Az \rightarrow (z = x \lor z = y)))$$

$$3A \leftrightarrow \exists x \exists y \exists z \, (Ax \,\&\, Ay \,\&\, Az \,\&\, x \neq y \,\&\, x \neq z \,\&\, y \neq z$$
$$\&\, \forall w \, (Aw \rightarrow (w = x \lor w = y \lor w = z)))$$

or more radically, like this:

$$1A \leftrightarrow \exists x \forall y \, (Ay \leftrightarrow y = x)$$

$$2A \leftrightarrow \exists x \exists y \, (x \neq y \,\&\, \forall z \, (Az \leftrightarrow (z = x \lor z = y)))$$

$$3A \leftrightarrow \exists x \exists y \exists z \, (x \neq y \,\&\, x \neq z \,\&\, y \neq z$$
$$\&\, \forall w \, (Aw \leftrightarrow (w = x \lor w = y \lor w = z)))$$

For each n, each of these three definitions of nA comes to the same thing, i.e., the three right-hand sides of the biconditionals are equivalent.

It was Bertrand Russell* who proposed the system of levels, together with the following restriction.

Type restriction: When one symbol is predicated of another, the one must belong to a higher level ("type") than the other.

Thus, in Example 1, the constants "0," "1," "2,". . . belong to level 2, while the variable "A" belongs to level 1 and the variables "x," "y," etc., belong to level 0, so that Russell's type restriction is satisfied when we write "$0A$," "Ax," etc. In Frege's formalization† of logic, where no such restriction was imposed, paradoxes arise. The simplest of these was discovered by Russell in 1901.¶

---

* "Mathematical Logic as Based on the Theory of Types," *American Journal of Mathematics*, **30**:222–262, 1908.
† Gottlob Frege, *Begriffsschrift*, Halle, 1879. Translated in Jan van Heijenoort (ed.), *From Frege to Gödel*, Harvard University Press, Cambridge, Mass., 1967.
¶ See "Letter to Frege" in van Heijenoort, op cit., pp. 124–125.

Example 2: Russell's Paradox

Plausibly, Frege assumed that any condition that can be formulated determines a predicate, applicable to the things that satisfy the condition. Example: The condition

$$-\exists x \, vLx$$

that is met by people v who love no one. The assumption that this condition determines a predicate, w, can be formulated as follows:

$$\exists w \forall v \, (wv \leftrightarrow -\exists x \, vLx)$$

That assumption is quite natural, and harmless. And in general it may seem harmless and natural to assume the comprehension axiom.

Comprehension axiom: Where $p[v]$ is any condition on v, the statement $\exists w \forall v \, (wv \leftrightarrow p[v])$ is true.

But not all statements of this form are true. Thus, suppose that $p[v]$ is the condition

$$-vv$$

of non-self-applicability. (Example: *Loves somebody* is a non-self-applicable predicate, for it is people, not predicates, who love.) Then non-self-applicability may seem to be a genuine predicate. But as Russell pointed out in a letter to Frege in 1902, a contradiction arises when we make that assumption, as the comprehension axiom would have us do.

> Let w be the predicate: to be a predicate that cannot be predicated of itself. Can w be predicated of itself? From each answer its opposite follows. Therefore we must conclude that w is not a predicate.*

* van Heijenoort, op. cit., p. 125.

1	$\sqrt{\exists w \forall v (wv \leftrightarrow -vv)}$	
2	$\forall v (av \leftrightarrow -vv)$	(from 1)
3	$\sqrt{(aa \leftrightarrow -aa)}$	(from 2)
4	$aa \qquad -aa$	(from 3)
5	$-aa \qquad --aa$	(from 3)
	$\times \qquad\quad \times$	

Figure 7-2 **Tree test for satisfiability of
"$\exists w \forall v (wv \leftrightarrow -vv)$."**

In other words, when we put "$-vv$" for $p[v]$ in the comprehension axiom, we obtain a statement

$$\exists w \forall v \ (wv \leftrightarrow -vv)$$

that cannot be true, for it is unsatisfiable: witness the tree test shown in Figure 7-2. Thus Frege's system is inconsistent in the absence of some such restriction as Russell's on the condition $p[v]$ in the comprehension axiom.

7-2 FIRST-ORDER INTERPRETATIONS

After that preliminary look at the larger context, we return to first-order logic in this section and Sections 7-3 through 7-7. Here we specify what "counterexample" is to mean in the "no counterexamples" definition of first-order validity, or (which comes to the same thing) what "interpretation" is to mean in the definition of first-order satisfiability as truth in some first-order interpretation.

Pending interpretation, statements in the notation of first-order logic are meaningless strings of marks. For the most part we have been interpreting such strings simply by supplying English translations, e.g., as follows:

$\forall x \exists y \ yLx$	Each is loved.
$\exists x \forall y \ xLy$	Some love all.
$\forall x \exists y \ (yLx \ \& \ \forall z \ yLz)$	Each is loved by some who love all.

But now it is time to be more systematic, e.g., to interpret these three statements by specifying a nonempty set D as the domain (of "individuals") over which the variables "x," "y," "z" range, and to specify in which pairs of individuals the first is supposed to love the second, in this interpretation.

The crucial fact is that the truth values of such complex statements are fixed, once it is determined what pairs of individuals the letter "L" is to be true of—no matter what it is about those pairs that *makes* "L" true of them. Thus, suppose that (as luck would have it) the pairs in which the first member *loves* the second are exactly those in which the first *has a lower taxpayer identification number than* the second. Then the truth values of "∀x∃y xLy," etc., would be the same, no matter which of these ways we use to identify the pairs. So for purposes of determining the truth values of statements in which they occur, we need not know what such symbols as "L" *mean*. It is enough if we know what pairs of individuals they are true of. The case was entirely similar in truth-functional logic, where we needed to know only the truth values (not the meanings) of statement letters in order to determine the truth values of compound statements built of them.

Then in surveying all interpretations of a set of statements in order to discover whether or not that set is satisfiable, we need not concern ourselves with meanings ("intensions") of symbols like "L." As we shall see, it will be enough to know the *extensions* of such symbols in the following sense.

INGREDIENTS IN A FIRST-ORDER INTERPRETATION

TYPE OF SYMBOL	EXTENSION
1. Quantifier	A nonempty set D of "individuals" (the same D for all individual quantifiers)
2. Name	An individual (i.e., a member of D)
3. Function symbol	An assignment of an individual to each n-tuple of individuals
4. Statement letter	A truth value
5. n-place predicate letter	A set of n-tuples of individuals

The quantifiers "∀x," "∃x," "∀y," "∃y," etc., share a common domain D, the specification of which is part of the business of specifying a particular first-order interpretation. Note that 1-tuples of individuals are simply individuals. Thus, the extension of a one-place predicate letter will simply be the set of members of D of which the predicate letter is true in the interpretation in question. The extensions of two-place (or three-place, etc.) predicate letters will be the sets of those pairs (or triples, etc.) of members of D of which those predicate letters are true in the interpretation.

The sign of identity "=" is a special two-place predicate letter—special in the sense that its extension is fully determined once the domain of individuals is chosen:

---

6. The extension of "=" is the set of all pairs (d, d) with d in D.

The symbol "i" for the identity function (see problem 8 at the end of Section 5-8) is also special in that same sense:

---

7. The extension of "i" is the assignment, to each individual, of that individual itself.

Thus choice of the domain D determines the extensions of all quantifiers and of the two symbols "=" and "i." When the other assignments of types 2 to 5 have been made, a first-order interpretation has been fully specified. That interpretation will determine truth values for all statements that can be formed from the symbols to which it assigns extensions by means of parentheses, variables, and connectives. Of course, symbols in categories 2 to 4 that appear in none of the statements whose truth values are of interest to us need not be assigned extensions, e.g., if no statement letters and no function symbols appear in those statements, no assignments of types 4 or 3 need be made.

7-3   RULES OF FORMATION

Now let us survey the forms that statements in first-order notation can have, with a view to seeing (in Section 7-4) how the truth values of statements of these forms are determined by the extensions of symbols that appear in them.

To begin, we shall need the following definition.

CONSTANTS (FOR INDIVIDUALS)

Names are constants. Other constants can be formed by writing constants in all places of function symbols, but in no other way.

Note that each function symbol has a definite number of places, whose number and location must be identified, either explicitly or as part of some background convention, before the function symbol can be said to have been identified. Thus, in the system Q of Robinson arithmetic (Example 19 of Chapter 5), we identified these three configurations of signs as function symbols:

$$\prime \qquad (\; + \;) \qquad (\; \cdot \;)$$

The first was identified as a one-place function symbol, with the one place just left of the accent, and the other two were identified as two-place function symbols, with the two places coming between the parentheses and the signs in the middle. There are similar requirements for predicate letters: in each case, the number of places must be specified, and there must be an understanding of where the places come. (We have been following the convention that where there are two places, they come just before and just after the letter, but that all places follow the letter when their number is not two.)

We can now define atomic statements:

ATOMIC STATEMENTS

Statement letters are atomic statements, and so are the results of writing constants in all places of predicate letters, but nothing else counts as an atomic statement.

These provide an initial stock of statements. Further statements are then obtainable by using truth-functional composition and generalization.

TRUTH-FUNCTIONAL COMPOSITION

Statements result when dashes are written before statements, and when statements are written in the blanks of these:

(→),(↔),(&),(∨),
(& &),(∨ ∨),...

That is as in truth-functional logic. The step to first-order logic comes when we *generalize*, e.g., when we form a statement "∀x xLa" that says about *everybody* what "*bLa*" says about *b*, or a statement "∃y∀x xLy" that says about an unspecified *somebody* what "∀x xLa" says about *a*:

GENERALIZATION*

∀*v* *p*[*v*] and ∃*v* *p*[*v*] are statements whenever *p*[*n*] is a statement in which the name *n* occurs but the variable *v* does not and *p*[*v*] is the result of replacing all the *n*'s in *p*[*n*] by *v*'s.

This completes our survey of the forms that statements can have in the notation of first-order logic.

The ways in which complex statements are formed from atomic ones can be displayed graphically by formation trees as follows.

Example 3: Two Formation Trees

Figure 7-3*a* is the formation tree for one of the premises of the inference with which we introduced universal generalization in Section 5-2 (Example 8). Figure 7-3*b* is for axiom Q3 of the system of Robinson arithmetic (Example 19 in Section 5-7).

---

*This form of the rule was suggested by George Boolos. It allows the corresponding rule of valuation to take the simple form (12) given in Section 7-4.

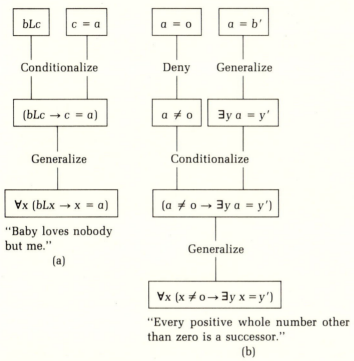

"Baby loves nobody but me."

(a)

"Every positive whole number other than zero is a successor."

(b)

Figure 7-3 Formation trees.

7-4 RULES OF VALUATION

Corresponding to the rules of formation in Section 7-3 are rules of valuation, specifying how the extensions of complex expressions are determined by the extensions of the components out of which they are formed. To begin, we must be given the basic ingredients of an interpretation I as described in Section 7-2. We now think of I as a function, assigning extensions $I(n)$, $I(p)$, etc., to names n, statement letters p, etc.

BASIC ASSIGNMENTS

   1. A domain of individuals $D = I(``\forall x") = I(``\exists x") = I(``\forall y") = \cdots$

   2. Individuals $I(n)$ as bearers (or "referents") of names n.

   3. For n-place function symbols s, functions $I(s)$ assigning individuals as values to n-tuples of individuals as arguments.

   4. Truth values $I(p)$ as extensions of statement letters p.

   5. Sets $I(P)$ of n-tuples of individuals as extensions of n-place predicate letters P.

The choice of a domain in 1 above determines the extension of the sign of identity:

SIGN OF IDENTITY

   6. $I(``=")$ is the set of all pairs (d, d) with d in D.

As we shall have no use for the identity function symbol "i," we shall not repeat 7 here.

Such are the values assigned by interpretation functions I to simple symbols. Now the following rules of valuation extend the domains of definition of those functions to compound symbols.

COMPOUND CONSTANTS (FOR INDIVIDUALS)

   8. $I(j) = \mathscr{F}(I(k_1), \ldots, I(k_n))$ if j is formed by writing constants $k_1, \ldots, k_n$ in the blanks of an n-place function symbol s, and $I(s) = \mathscr{F}$.

The constants $k_1, \ldots, k_n$ themselves may be compound, but if so, they have fewer components than j, and a finite number in all. Then after some finite number of applications of this rule we shall reach a point at which all the remaining k's are simple names.

COMPOUND ATOMIC STATEMENTS

   9. If p is an atomic statement formed by writing constants $k_1, \ldots, k_n$ in the successive places of an n-place predicate letter P, then $I(p)$ is t or f depending on whether or not the n-tuple $(I(k_1), \ldots, I(k_n))$ is in the set $I(P)$.

It only remains to consider nonatomic statements. For truth-functional compounds, the rules of valuation are familiar from the first four chapters, e.g., for denial and the conditional:

TRUTH-FUNCTIONAL COMPOUNDS

    10. a If q is formed by writing a dash before the statement p, then $I(q)$ is f or t depending on whether $I(p)$ is t or f.

          b If r is formed by writing statements p and q in the successive blanks of ($\rightarrow$), then $I(r) = $ t if $I(p) = $ f or $I(q) = $ t, and $I(r) = $ f if $I(p) = $ t and $I(q) = $ f.

The rules of valuation for generalizations are stated in terms of interpretations I_d^n that differ slightly from the given interpretation I:

NOMINAL VARIANTS OF INTERPRETATIONS

    11. I_d^n is the interpretation that assigns d to n ($I_d^n(n) = $ d) but otherwise makes the same basic assignments as I.

If it happens that $I(n) = $ d, then I_d^n will be the same interpretation as I. Notice that the process of variation described in 11 can be iterated, e.g., I_{de}^{nm} will be the assignment that differs from I_d^n (if at all) in that it assigns e to m. Thus it differs from I (if at all) in that it assigns d to n and e to m.

In case I assigns no interpretation to n, I_d^n will extend I—making the same assignments that I does, but *also* assigning d to n. Now as d ranges over the domain D, the truth values $I_d^n(p[n])$ that I_d^n assigns to $p[n]$ may vary or not. Perhaps $p[n]$ is true in each such interpretation. If so, the universal generation $\forall v\, p[v]$ will be true in I, but if $p[n]$ is false for even one individual d in D, then the universal generalization will be false in I. Similarly, the existential generalization $\exists v\, p[v]$ will be true in I if $p[n]$ is true in even one of the interpretations I_d^n, and will be false in I if $p[n]$ is false in all those variants of I. Then we can formulate the rule of valuation for generalizations:

GENERALIZATIONS

    12. Choose a name n to which I assigns no bearer.

        a $I(\forall v\, p[v] = $ t iff for each d in D, $I_d^n(p[n]) = $ t.

        b $I(\exists v\, p[v]) = $ t iff for some d in D, $I_d^n(p[n]) = $ t.

The rules of valuation are now complete. We illustrate their application in the case of the statements whose formation trees were shown in Example 3.

Example 4: "Baby Loves Nobody but Me"

We describe an interpretation I in which the translation "$\forall x \ (bLx \rightarrow x = a)$" of this statement is true. First, the basic ingredients.

1. $I("\forall x") = D = $ a set consisting of several people, among whom are two distinct people, viz., *baby* and *me*.

2. $I("a") = me$ and $I("b") = baby$.

5. $I("L")$ is a set of pairs, among which is the pair ($baby$, me), but no other pairs of form ($baby$, d).

There are no other basic assignments. In particular, I assigns no bearer to the name "c," which can thus play the role of $\boldsymbol{n}$ in 12. We now calculate $I("\forall x \ (bLx \rightarrow x = a)")$ in stages, working our way up the first valuation tree in Example 3 and applying the appropriate rules as we move from box to box: see Figure 7-4 (where the tree is shown upside down). Since either $d \neq me$ or $d = me$ for each d in D, $I("\forall x \ (bLx \rightarrow x = a)") = t$.

Figure 7-4

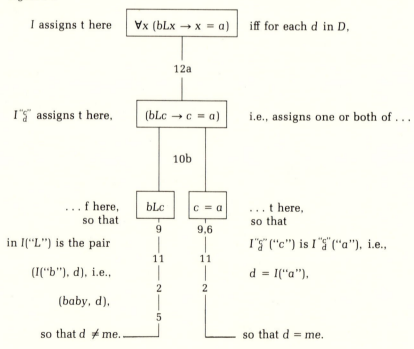

Example 5: "Every Positive Whole Number Other Than 0 Is a Successor"

We calculate the truth value of the translation "$\forall x\,(x \neq o \rightarrow \exists y\,x = y')$" of this statement in the interpretation I that has these basic ingredients and no others:

1. $I("\forall x") = I("\exists y") = D =$ the set consisting of 0, 1, 2, ...

2. $I("o") = 0$.

3. $I("\ '\ ") =$ the sucessor function, $1+$.

The remaining steps are given in Figure 7-5.

   Then the complex statement is true if $d = 0$ (lower left), and also if $d = 1 + e$ for some e (lower right). Then the complex statement is true, for each d satisfies one or the other of these conditions.

Figure 7-5

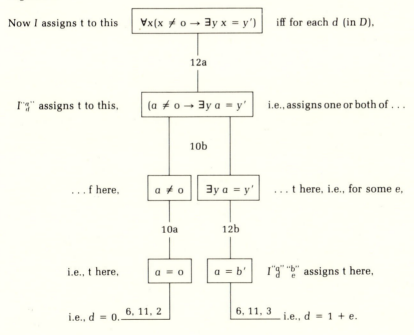

Now I assigns t to this $\forall x(x \neq o \rightarrow \exists y\,x = y')$ iff for each d (in D),

12a

$I\,{}^{"a"}_{d}$ assigns t to this, $(a \neq o \rightarrow \exists y\,a = y'$ i.e., assigns one or both of . . .

10b

. . . f here, $a \neq o$ $\exists y\,a = y'$ . . . t here, i.e., for some e,

10a   12b

i.e., t here, $a = o$ $a = b'$ $I\,{}^{"a"}_{d}\,{}^{"b"}_{e}$ assigns t here,

i.e., $d = 0$.   6, 11, 2   6, 11, 3   i.e., $d = 1 + e$.

7-5 VALIDITY CORRECTNESS

We now prove that whenever the tree test classifies an inference as valid (or classifies a set of statements as unsatisfiable), that classification is correct. This is a matter of demonstrating that *if all paths in a tree are closed, the initial list of statements is unsatisfiable*, or, what comes to the same thing:

"SOUNDNESS" THEOREM

If the initial list is satisfiable, there will be an open path through any (finished or unfinished) tree that is obtainable from that list.

The term "soundness" is put in scare quotes above because it is being used in a different sense from that introduced in Section 1-4. There it was applied to inferences and meant *valid and with all premises true*. Here it is applied to a method for testing validity of inferences and means *reliable to this extent*: if the method classifies an inference as valid, then the inference really is valid. (The term "validity correctness" suggests this more clearly, but the term "soundness" is more commonly used.) The other sort of reliability— invalidity correctness—is commonly called "completeness." That will be discussed in Section 7-6. The remainder of this section is devoted to a proof of the soundness theorem.

To prove the soundness theorem it suffices to prove that *if the initial list is satisfiable, so is some path through each (finished or unfinished) tree that is obtainable from it.* (A satisfiable path is one whose full lines form a satisfiable set. Then a satisfiable path cannot be closed, i.e., it cannot contain a statement and its denial as full lines.) And to prove that, it suffices to prove the soundness lemma:

SOUNDNESS LEMMA

Whenever a rule of inference is applied to a statement or pair of statements in a satisfiable path, there will be at least one list of conclusions that (added to the path) yields a satisfiable longer path.

The rules of inference in question are those for the connectives, the quantifiers, and the sign of identity "=." We continue to ignore the identity function symbol "i" (see 7 in Section 7-2), and to avoid pointless complications, we also ignore all connectives except for the expressively complete pair consisting of "→" and "−." Then there

$-p$	$\sqrt{(p \to q)}$	$j = k$	q has k (or j) at one or more places where p has j (or k)	$\dfrac{\forall v\, p[v]}{p[k]}$	$\dfrac{\sqrt{\exists v\, p[v]}}{p[n]}$
$\dfrac{p}{\times}$	$\overline{-p \mid q}$	$\dfrac{p}{q}$			$\uparrow$ a new name
Denial	Conditional	Identity		UI	EI
$\dfrac{\sqrt{-\,-p}}{p}$	$\dfrac{\sqrt{-(p \to q)}}{\begin{array}{c}p\\ -q\end{array}}$	$\dfrac{k \neq k}{\times}$		$\dfrac{\sqrt{-\forall v\, p}}{\exists v - p}$	$\dfrac{\sqrt{-\exists v\, p}}{\forall v - p}$
Double denial	Denied conditional	Diversity (denied identity)		Denied quantifiers	

Figure 7-6   **Rules of inference.**

are 10 rules in all; see Figure 7-6. In UI and in the rules for identity and diversity, k (and j) can be any constant.

Now to prove the lemma (and thus the theorem), we need only verify that whenever all statements appearing as full lines in some path are true in some interpretation I with domain D, and a rule of inference is applied to a line or pair of lines in that path, at least one list of conclusions, added to the path, will yield a longer path in which all lines are true either in I itself or (if the rule was UI) in some nominal variant I^n_d of I (where n is the new name used in EI); see Figure 7-7. We verify this claim by considering the rules of inference in groups.

Figure 7-7

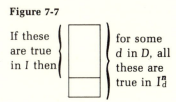

If these are true in I then { } for some d in D, all these are true in I^n_d

Group 1: The rules for denial and diversity. These are the rules for closing ("×") paths. Here the claim is true because when either rule is applicable to a line or a pair of lines in a path, there will be no interpretation I in which that premise or those premises are true, and thus no interpretation in which all full lines in the path are true. In the case of the rule for denial, this is verified by 10a, according to which one of $I(p)$, $I(-p)$ must be f. In the case of the rule for diversity, it is verified by 6, according to which the pair $(I(k), I(k))$ must be in $I("=")$; 9 according to which $I("k = k")$ must then be t; and 10a, according to which $I("k \neq k")$ must then be f.

Group 2: The rest of the rules except for EI. Each of these may be applicable to a line or pair of lines in a path in which all full lines are true in an interpretation I, but in any such case, the conclusion (or, in the rule for the conditional, a conclusion) will also be true in I. For the three truth-functional rules, this claim is straightforwardly verifiable by 10; for the rule for identity, by 6 and 9; and for the rules for denied quantifiers, by 10a, 12, and 11. Here, e.g., is the verification in the case of the rule for $-\forall$: $I(-\forall v\, p[v]) = $ t iff (by 10a) $I(\forall v\, p[v]) \neq $ t iff (by 12a) $I_d^n (p[n]) = $ f for some d in D iff (by 10a) $I_d^n(-p[n]) = $ t for some d in D iff (by 12b) $I(\exists v\, -p[v]) = $ t.

Group 3: The rule for EI. If all full lines in a path are true in I and one of those lines has form $\exists v\, p[v]$, then by 12b, $I_d^n(p[n]) = $ t for some d in D, QED.

7-6 COMPLETENESS (INVALIDITY CORRECTNESS)

The converse of the "soundness" theorem asserts that *if the initial list is unsatisfiable, then all paths through the finished tree are closed*, or, what comes to the same thing:

COMPLETENESS THEOREM

If there is an open path through every tree that is obtainable from an initial list, then that list is satisfiable.

In effect, this theorem claims ("invalidity correctness") that *if the tree method classifies an inference as invalid* (or classifies a set of statements as satisfiable), *then that classification is correct.* Putting this in an equivalent, contrapositive form, we have a claim that the tree test for validity is *complete:* that whenever an inference really is valid (or a set of statements really is unsatisfiable), the tree test classifies it so. As in the case of validity correctness in Section 7-5, we confine ourselves to the straightforward case where the inference has only finitely many premises (perhaps none, i.e., perhaps we are testing validity of a single statement). This restriction is evident in the boxed formulation of the theorem, for the initial list must be finite. The soundness and completeness theorems have stronger versions in which the finiteness restriction is removed, but the weak forms suffice for our present purposes.

Similarly, for the purpose of proving Gödel's incompleteness theorem in Section 7-9, it will not be necessary to have proved completeness of the tree method for all inferences in first-order notation; we can exclude inferences in which there appear statement letters, or function symbols, or the sign of identity "=." As the proof is shorter and clearer when these restrictive assumptions are made, we now prove the restricted form of the completeness theorem in which these three sorts of items are excluded from the basic notation.

We shall reason in terms of *complete* trees, to which the rules of inference are no longer applicable. In the case of trees that never stop growing (e.g., the tree that is generated when we test satisfiability of the statement "$\forall x \exists y\ xLy$"), the complete tree is never before us on paper, for at no finite stage in the business of applying rules do we reach a point at which no rule is applicable. Still, we can discuss the infinite tree that would be generated by endlessly applying the *tree program*, for which a (slightly sketchy) flow diagram is provided in Figure 7-8. (To fill in all details, we would have to be

Figure 7-8   The tree program, in outline.

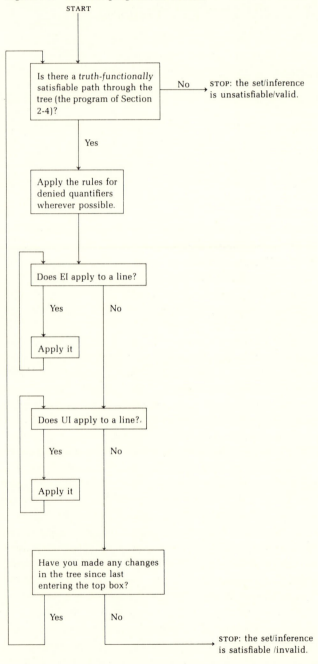

$\forall x\,Ax$	p	$\forall x\,Ax$	p
$(\forall x\,Ax \rightarrow \forall x\,Bx)$	$(p \rightarrow q)$	$\forall x\,(Ax \rightarrow Bx)$	r
$\forall x\,Bx$	q	$\forall x\,Bx$	q

(a) Truth-functionally valid   (b) Truth-functionally invalid

Figure 7-9   Two valid inferences and their truth-functional forms.

quite explicit about the order of application of rules in cases where the order is quite unimportant, e.g., we would have to say which of the two rules for denied quantifiers is to be applied first.) The program is specified in enough detail to guarantee that if there is any order of application of the rules of inference that makes all paths close, then any order of application that conforms to the flow diagram will eventually extrude us from that program on the upper STOP arrow with all paths closed.

Concerning the two exits from the top box in Figure 7-8, notice that although both of the inferences shown in Figure 7-9 will be classified correctly as valid by the present (first-order) tree test, the first of them is *truth-functionally* valid (so that the question in the top box gets the answer "no" the first time it is asked), but the second is not (so that we shall leave that box through the "yes" arrow on our first pass, to get the answer "no" only the second time the question is asked).

We now prove the completeness theorem.

Suppose (see the "if" clause in the statement of the theorem) that in applying the tree program, starting with a certain initial list, we never leave the top box through the right-hand, STOP arrow. There are two possibilities. (1) We do eventually leave the program through the STOP arrow at the bottom of the graph, so that the finished tree is finite. (2) We never leave the program, i.e., we go around the big loop (leftmost arrow) no end of times, so that the complete tree (of which we see a larger initial part every time we go around the big loop) is infinite. In either case, *there will be an open path through the complete tree.* [In case 2 this follows from König's lemma (Section 3-8), according to which there is an infinite path through any infinite tree. An infinite path must be open, for a path that contains an "×" at some point must terminate there, and thus be finite.]

Now, given an open path through the complete tree, we define an interpretation I as follows. (We need only specify the basic ingredients of types 1, 2, and 5, since no statement letters or function symbols appear in the initial list.)

1. The domain D of the interpretation is either the set of all the positive whole numbers (in case no end of different names appear in the path) or the set consisting of the first u of them, where u is the (finite) number of distinct names that appear in the path.

2. I assigns positive whole numbers 1, 2, . . . in turn as bearers of the distinct names that appear in the path, in order of first appearance. (Statement letters are excluded from the notation, so that if no names appear in the initial list, at least one will appear in the path by means of an application of UI or EI.)

5. For each predicate letter P that appears in the path (with, say, n places), $I(P)$ is the set consisting of those n-tuples $(d_1, \ldots, d_n)$ whose names occupy the successive places of P in an atomic statement that appears as a full line of the path.

Thus, in testing validity of the invalid inference from "aLa" to "bLa," the names that appear in the one-path tree are "a" and "b" in order of first appearance, so that D will have just the two members $I("a") = 1$ and $I("b") = 2$; and as the only full lines of the path will be "aLa" and "$-bLa$," the extension $I("L")$ of "L" will be the set having the pair (1, 1) as its solitary member.

To prove the completeness theorem, we show that all full lines of the path are true in the interpretation I that we have just defined. The proof uses the fact on which mathematical induction is based: *any nonempty set of positive whole numbers has a smallest member.* Then the set of lengths of lines in the path that are not true in I must have a smallest member or be empty. We shall deduce a contradiction from the supposition that the set has a smallest member, and thus prove that it is empty, i.e., that all full lines of the path are true in I.

Suppose then that I (which assigns truth values to *all* lines of the path) assigns f to at least one line. Then there will be one or more shortest such lines. Let p be one of the shortest: $I(p) = $ f, but $I(q) = $ t for every shorter line q in the path. We now verify that p cannot have any of the nine forms that statements are capable of having in the allowed notation. (To avoid pointless complications, we take "$\rightarrow$" and "$-$" to be the only connectives.)

Form 1: p is atomic. Then *p* is true, by 5 above (and 9 of Section 7-4). Thus *I(p)* cannot be f, after all.

Form 2: p is of form −q, where q is atomic. Then by 5 (and 9 of Section 7-4), *I(q)* must be f [as *q* cannot also be in the (open) path], and so *p* cannot have been a shortest false line.

Form 3: p is of form −−q. Then the rule for double denial will have been applied (as the tree is complete), and *q* itself will be in the path, i.e., a statement shorter than *p* but with the same truth value, i.e., f. Then *p* cannot have been one of the shortest false lines.

Form 4: p is of form (q → r). Then the rule for conditionals will have been applied to *p*, and either the denial −*q* of the antecedent, or the consequent *r*, will be a line of the path. As each of these is shorter than *p*, the one in the path must be true in *I*; and as each of them implies the conditional *p*, *I(p)* cannot be f, after all.

Form 5: p is of form −(q → r). Then the rule for denied conditionals will have been applied to *p*, and so both *q* and −*r* will be in the path. Being shorter than *p*, each of these must be true in *I*; and as, together, they imply *p*, *I(p)* cannot be f, after all.

Form 6: p is of form ∀v q[v]. Then UI will have been applied to *p* once for each name *n* that appears in the path. Each of these conclusions *q[n]* will be shorter than *p*, and hence true in *I*. But by 1 and 2 above, the bearers *I(n)* of these names will exhaust *D*, and thus, by 12a and 11 of Section 7-4, *I(p)* will be t after all.

Form 7: p is of form ∃v q[v]. Then EI will have been applied to *p*, unless there was already some line in the path of form *q[n]*. Then there will be a line of that form in the path, shorter than *p* (and thus t in *I*) and implying *p* (so that *p* must also be t in *I*, after all).

Form 8: p is of form −∀v r. Then the relevant rule for denied quantifiers will have been applied to *p*, and there will be a line in the path of form ∃v −*r*, of the same length as *p*. But we have just shown that to be impossible (in the treatment of form 7, with −*r* as *q[v]*).

Form 9: p is of form −∃v r. Then the relevant rule for denied quantifiers will have been applied to *p*, and there will be a line in the path of form ∀v −*r*, of the same length as *p*. But we have shown that to be impossible (in the treatment of form 6, with −*r* as *q[v]*).

Then *p* cannot have any of the nine forms that statements can have. There is no shortest line in the path to which *I* assigns f, i.e., *I(p)* = t for every line *p* in the path. The completeness theorem is proved.

7-7 LÖWENHEIM'S THEOREM*

If all statements in a set (or a list or a path) are true in an interpretation I, then I is said to *satisfy* the set (list, path) and to be a *model* of it. If the domain of I is D, then the set (etc.) is said to be *satisfiable in D* and to have a *model in D*. Thus, in Section 7-6 we proved the completeness theorem for first-order logic by showing that any open path through a finished tree determines a model of the initial list in a domain of positive integers; see part 1 of the definition of I there.

By tinkering with that construction, we can prove the Löwenheim theorem:

LÖWENHEIM'S THEOREM

For finite sets of statements in first-order notation without function symbols or the sign of identity: *if they are satisfiable at all, they are satisfiable in the domain of all positive integers.*

Some of the restrictions in this form of the theorem are inessential, e.g., the set need not be finite (the theorem also holds for sets containing as many statements as there are positive integers), nor need we exclude function symbols from the notation. With those restrictions the proof is simpler, and the theorem is no less useful as a step toward the proof of Gödel's incompleteness theorem in Section 7-8. But the exclusion of the identity sign "$=$" is essential, for by using that sign we can easily formulate statements that are satisfiable in interpretations with finite domains, but in none with infinite domains. The simplest example is the statement

$$\forall x \forall y \; x = y$$

which is true in all interpretations with one-member domains, and in none with larger domains.

Now to prove Löwenheim's theorem we observe (1) that if the program of Section 7-6 generates an infinite tree, there is nothing to prove, and (2) that if the program does not generate an infinite tree, we can always pad the list so that it does, with the desired effect. Both points need explanation—especially the second.

---

* This thoerem (also called the "Löwenheim-Skolem" theorem) was proved by Leopold Löwenheim in 1915. In 1920 it was generalized by Thoralf Skolem, who also simplified the proof. The original papers are translated in Jean van Heijenoort, *From Frege to Gödel,* Harvard University Press, Cambridge, Mass., 1967.

1. If the tree is infinite, then it contains an open path in which no end of different names appear, and therefore (see item 1 in the definition of I in Section 7-6) the domain of I is the set of all positive integers. As all lines of the initial list are true in I, they are seen to be satisfiable in the domain stipulated by the theorem.

2. If the finished tree is finite, we choose some predicate letter that appears in the initial list, write v's in all its places to get $p[v]$, do the same thing with w's to get $p[w]$, and add this statement to the initial list as a new line:

$$\forall v \exists w \, (p[v] \rightarrow p[w])$$

As can easily be verified by the tree test, this statement will be valid, and so the new, padded list will have the same models as the original list. But the $\forall \exists$ form of the new line ensures that the program will generate an infinite tree from the padded initial list, if the original list was satisfiable.

This completes the proof of Löwenheim's theorem.

Before going on, let us pause to note the unimportance of the fact that the domain D of the interpretation associated with the infinite path has been identified as the *set of all positive integers* in particular, and not as some other set whose members can be enumerated in an unending list without repetitions. The set we chose for the role of D is enumerable as suggested in the first row of Figure 7-10, but each of the other rows indicates an enumeration of that or some other set that would serve our purpose just as well. That purpose is simply to allow us to *assign bearers to names in their order of appearance in the path* (see 2 in Section 7-6): the first member of D as enumerated is assigned as bearer to the first name

Figure 7-10 Some enumerably infinite sets.

1,	2,	3,	4,	. . .
0,	1,	2,	3,	. . .
−1,	−2,	−3,	−4,	. . .
2,	4,	6,	8,	. . .
1,	10,	100,	1000,	. . .
1,	0.1,	0.01,	0.001,	. . .
1,	−1,	2,	−2,	. . .
2,	1,	4,	3,	. . .

to appear, the second member to the second name, and so on. As two lines of the (satisfiable) path may have forms $p[n]$ and $-p[m]$, it is important that distinct names have distinct bearers; to avoid ambiguity, it is important that distinct bearers have distinct names (so that $I(n)$ will be single-valued); to avoid gaps that might prevent EI from working as intended, it is important that each name in the path have a bearer in D; and to ensure the completeness that is needed to make the point about form 6 ($\forall v\, q[v]$) in Section 7-6, it is important that all members of D have names in the path.

To ensure all that, it was necessary and sufficient that it be possible to pair off names n in the path with members d of D exhaustively, in a 1-to-1 manner, by the relation

$$I(n) = d$$

And to ensure that, it is necessary and sufficient that the set D be enumerably infinite (or "denumerable") in the sense that its members can be arranged in a single, unending list

$$d_0, d_1, d_2, \ldots$$

in which each member of D appears just once, sooner or later. To be more abstract, the requirement is that there be a two-place relation S ("is immediately succeeded by") corresponding to such a list: d_i bears S to d_j iff j is $i + 1$. Where the variables range over D, the requirement is that the assignments

$$I(\text{"o"}) = d_0$$

and

$$I(\text{"S"}) = \text{the set of all pairs } (d_i, d_{i+1}) \text{ with } d_i \text{ in } D$$

determine an interpretation in which all five of the statements in Figure 7-11 are true.

$\forall x \exists y \, xSy$	Everything has a successor.
$\forall x \forall y \forall z \, ((zSx \,\&\, zSy) \rightarrow x = y)$	Nothing has two distinct successors.
$\forall x \forall y \forall z \, ((xSz \,\&\, ySz) \rightarrow x = y)$	No two things have the same successor.
$\forall x \, \neg xSo$	o is not a successor.
$\forall P \, ((Po \,\&\, \forall x \forall y \, ((Px \,\&\, xSy) \rightarrow Py)) \rightarrow \forall x \, Px)$ Anything true of o, and true of the successors of all the things it is true of, is true of everything.	

Figure 7-11   A domain is enumerably infinite iff this set is satisfiable in it.

Understanding a domain to be *enumerably infinite* (or *denumerable*) when the set of statements in Figure 7-11 is satisfiable in it, we can replace the reference to the domain of all positive integers in our statement of Löwenheim's theorem by a more general reference to any enumerably infinite domain.

> LÖWENHEIM'S THEOREM REFORMULATED
>
> For satisfiable finite sets of statements in first-order notation without function symbols or the sign of identity: they are *satisfiable in any enumerably infinite domain.*

Any of the eight enumerably infinite sets indicated above would do, as would no end of others, including sets whose members are not numbers. (One such possibility is the set of all *names* that appear in the path, with each name *n* being assigned itself as bearer: $I(n) = n$.)

But note: The fifth of our defining conditions for enumerable infinity takes us outside the bounds of first-order logic, as it contains a quantified predicate variable "P." We have not yet formulated explicit rules of valuation for such statements.

7-8   SECOND-ORDER FORMATION AND VALUATION RULES

First-order logic allows generalization of individual variables but of no predicate variables. In general, nth-order logic allows generalization of variables that range over levels *below* the nth. Thus, second-order logic uses not only the individual quantifiers "$\forall x$," "$\exists x$," "$\forall y$," etc., but also quantifiers "$\forall P$," " $\exists P$," "$\forall Q$," etc., where "P," "Q," etc., are predicate variables.

For our purposes in Section 7-9 it will be convenient to count all first-order statements as second-order statements as well, and then to get predicate variables simply by reclassifying certain predicate letters, pressing them into service as needed. *Example:* If we reclassify "K" as a predicate variable, then we can existentially generalize the statement

Alma knows no one who loves the Baron. $\forall x\ (xLb \rightarrow -aKx)$

to obtain the weaker, second-order statement

There is a relation that Alma bears to no one who loves the Baron.
$$\exists K\ \forall x\ (xLb \rightarrow -aKx)$$

This allows us to convert the rules of formation for first-order logic into an adequate set of rules of formation for second-order logic simply by adding these two.

SECOND-ORDER HEGEMONY (FORMATION)

   All first-order formation rules are duplicated as second-order formation rules.

Thus, if "a" and "b" are names and "L" is a two-place predicate letter, then "$(bLb \rightarrow -aLb)$" now counts as a statement in the notation of second-order logic.

SECOND-ORDER GENERALIZATIONS (FORMATION)

   $\forall Vp$ and $\exists Vp$ are second-order statements whenever p is a second-order statement in which the predicate letter V occurs but the quantifiers $\forall V$ and $\exists V$ do not.

And that completes the roster of forms that statements can have in the part of second-order logic that we shall be dealing with. *We continue to exclude function symbols and the sign of identity from first-order notation, and thus from second-order notation as well.*

The rules of valuation for second-order logic are the first-order rules, taken over wholesale, together with one more, corresponding to rules 11 and 12 for first-order generalizations.

SECOND-ORDER HEGEMONY (VALUATION)

All first-order valuation rules are duplicated as second-order valuation rules.

SECOND-ORDER GENERALIZATIONS (VALUATION)

13. a $I(\forall V \boldsymbol{p}) = \text{t}$ iff $I_E^V(\boldsymbol{p}) = \text{t}$ for *each* suitable extension E.

b $I(\exists V \boldsymbol{p}) = \text{t}$ iff $I_E^V(\boldsymbol{p}) = \text{t}$ for *some* suitable extension E.

If V is an n-place predicate letter, the *suitable extensions* will be the various sets of n-tuples of members of D. I_E^V is I itself if $I(V) = E$. If not, I_E^V is the interpretation determined by the same basic assignments 1, 2, 5 as those for I except that I_E^V assigns E to V.

We can now investigate various questions of validity and equivalence, e.g., we can verify that loss of the sign of identity from the basic notation brings with it no loss of expressive power, as identity is definable as follows in second-order notation.

Example 6: Leibniz's Law

The universally quantified biconditional "$\forall P\ (Pa \leftrightarrow Pb)$" is equivalent to the identity statement "$a = b$." Indeed, as A. N. Whitehead and Bertrand Russell pointed out in 1910,* we can weaken the biconditional to a conditional without sacrificing equivalence:

$I(\text{``}a\text{''}) = I(\text{``}b\text{''})$ if and only if $I(\text{``}\forall P\ (Pa \to Pb)\text{''}) = \text{t}$.

This is true for every interpretation I that assigns values to "a" and "b."

---

* *Principia Mathematica*, Cambridge University Press, Cambridge, England, vol. 1, 1910, p. 57.

Proof. The thought is that among a's properties is identity with a, so that if b has all a's properties, it must have that one, and thus must be identical with a. Then $I("a = b") = t$ if $I("\forall P\ (Pa \rightarrow Pb)") = t$. Proof of the converse is trivial. We now go through the proof minutely, to show how the various rules of valuation are used. We begin with the nontrivial ("if") direction.

Suppose that $I("\forall P\ (Pa \rightarrow Pb)") = t$. Then by 13, $\Gamma_E^{P}\ ("(Pa \rightarrow Pb)") = t$ for all suitable E, and so in particular for the set E that contains $I("a")$ and nothing else. Now by 10b, $I("Pa") = f$ or $I("Pb") = t$, and by 9 and the fact that $I("a")$ is in E, $I("Pa")$ is t, not f. Then it must be that $I("Pb") = t$, i.e., by 9, $I("b")$ is in E, i.e., $I("b") = I("a")$.

In the "only if" direction, the theorem is proved as follows.

Suppose that $I("a") = I("b")$. Then for all subsets E of D, $I("a")$ is in E iff $I("b")$ is in E, and so by 9 $\Gamma_E^{P}("Pa") = \Gamma_E^{P}("Pb")$, whence, by 10b, $\Gamma_E^{P}\ ("(Pa \rightarrow Pb)") = t$. As this is so for all suitable E, $I("\forall P(Pa \rightarrow Pb)") = t$ by 13.

This means that in the second and third of the statements in Figure 7-11 that are jointly satisfiable in all enumerably infinite domains, and in no others, we can eliminate the sign of identity "$=$" by using Leibniz's law; e.g., in place of the first of those statements

$$\forall x \forall y \forall z\ ((zSx\ \&\ zSy) \rightarrow x = y)$$

we can put this:

$$\forall x \forall y \forall z\ ((zSx\ \&\ zSy) \rightarrow \forall P\ (Px \rightarrow Py))$$

to the same effect; the two are true in exactly the same interpretations. Then in this restricted second-order notation (without "$=$" or function signs), we can formulate a statement den that is true in exactly those interpretations whose domains are denumerable (i.e., enumerably infinite). This will be the result of conjoining the five statements listed in Figure 7-11, then replacing the name "o" by a variable "w," and finally, existentially generalizing both "w" and "S."

THE STATEMENT den:

$\exists w \exists S (\forall x \exists y\ xSy\ \&$
$\qquad \forall x \forall y \forall z\ ((zSx\ \&\ zSy) \rightarrow \forall P\ (Px \rightarrow Py))\ \&$
$\qquad \forall x \forall y \forall z\ ((xSz\ \&\ ySz) \rightarrow \forall P\ (Px \rightarrow Py))\ \&$
$\qquad \forall x\ -xSw\ \&$
$\qquad \forall P\ ((Pw\ \&\ \forall x \forall y\ ((Px\ \&\ xSy) \rightarrow Py)) \rightarrow \forall x\ Px))$

den is true in I iff the domain of I is denumerable.

7-9 GÖDEL'S INCOMPLETENESS THEOREM

We now prove a form of Kurt Gödel's (1931) incompleteness theorem:

INCOMPLETENESS OF SECOND-ORDER LOGIC

Unsolvable: The problem of designing a sound, complete clerical routine for recognizing second-order validity.

We lose no generality by confining discussion to validity of statements, for validity of an inference with finitely many premises comes to the same thing as validity of the conditional statement having the conjunction of the premises as antecedent and having the conclusion as consequent. Recall that soundness/completeness of a routine for recognizing a property of statements is a matter of never committing sins of commission/omission in attributing that property to statements.

In contrast, first-order logic is complete:

COMPLETENESS OF FIRST-ORDER LOGIC

Solvable: The problem of designing a sound, complete clerical routine for recognizing first-order validity.

This was demonstrated in Section 7-6 by proving that the tree method is such a routine. But as we saw in Chapter 6, neither the tree method nor any other sound clerical routine for recognizing first-order *invalidity* is complete:

UNSOLVABILITY OF THE DECISION PROBLEM
FOR FIRST-ORDER VALIDITY

Unsolvable: The problem of designing a sound, complete clerical routine for recognizing first-order invalidity.

(Strictly speaking, the decision problem for first-order validity is the problem of designing *two* sound, complete clerical routines: one for presence and one for absence of validity. But in view of the completeness theorem, that problem is solvable or not depending on whether or not the problem about absence of validity is solvable.)

We shall prove Gödel's incompleteness theorem by reducing the halting problem for abacus programs to the problem of designing a sound, complete clerical routine for recognizing second-order validity, i.e., we shall prove that if there were such a routine, the halting problem would be solvable. (Similarly, in Chapter 6 we showed the decision problem for first-order validity to be unsolvable by reducing the halting problem to *it*.) Specifically, we shall prove Gödel's theorem by providing a clerical routine that can be applied to any abacus program A_n to yield a second-order statement p_n^* that is valid iff the program never halts.

Here are the instructions for finding p_n^*, given A_n.

a. As in Example 4 of Chapter 6 (at the end of Section 6-8), find a set of first-order statements (without function symbols but with identity) whose joint satisfiability comes to the same thing as invalidity of the "new-style" inference associated with A_n. (The set consists of the premises of the inference, together with the denials of the components of its disjunctive conclusion. See Figure 6-20a.)

b. In this set, replace the statement

$$\forall x \forall y \forall z \, ((xSy \, \& \, xSz) \rightarrow y = z)$$

(i.e., the second premise) by the statement

$$\forall x \forall y \forall z \, ((xSy \, \& \, xSz) \rightarrow \forall P \, (Py \rightarrow Pz))$$

to which it is equivalent by Leibniz's law.

c. Form the conjunction p_n of the statements in the set, i.e., a second-order statement free of "=" and function symbols (and statement letters), but containing the name "o" and the predicate letters "S" and "R."

d. Existentially generalize all names and predicate letters that appear in p_n. This is a matter of replacing "o" by an individual variable (perhaps "t") that does not appear in the conjunction, reclassifying "S" and "R" as variables, and writing "$\exists t \exists S \exists R$" at the left. Let us call the result "ex(p_n)."

e. Finally, form the conditional

$$den \rightarrow ex(p_n)$$

i.e., p_n^*. (Here, *den* is the statement shown in the box at the end of Section 7-8.)

Example 7: Finding $\text{ex}(\boldsymbol{p}_3)$

For the program A_3 (shown in Figure 6-11), the set referred to in instruction a consists of seven statements as shown in Example 4 of Chapter 6. Instructions b and c are straightforward, and the outcome of instruction d is the statement $\text{ex}(\boldsymbol{p}_3)$, i.e.,

$$\exists t \exists S \exists R \ (\forall x \exists y \ xSy \ \& \ \forall x \forall y \forall z \ ((xSy \ \& \ xSz) \rightarrow \forall P \ (Py \rightarrow Pz)) \ \& \ Rttt \ \&$$
$$\forall x \forall y \forall z \ ((xSy \ \& \ tSz \ \& \ Rxtt) \rightarrow Ryzt) \ \&$$
$$\forall x \forall y \forall u \forall v \forall w \forall z \ ((ySu \ \& \ xSv \ \& \ tSw \ \& \ wSz \ \& \ Rxtu) \rightarrow Rvzy) \ \&$$
$$\forall x \forall y \forall z \ (tSz \rightarrow -Rxzy) \ \& \ \forall x \forall y \forall z \forall w \ ((tSz \ \& \ zSw) \rightarrow -R\acute{x}wy))$$

The foregoing instructions specify a clerical routine for producing $\boldsymbol{p}_n^*$ given A_n. Then to prove Gödel's incompleteness theorem it only remains to show the following:

> $\boldsymbol{p}_n^*$ is valid iff A_n never halts.

It is understood that initially all registers are empty. The proof has three steps: it is a matter of showing that each of conditions 1, 2, and 3 below is equivalent to the condition that follows it.

1. A_n never halts (after being started with all registers empty).

2. $\boldsymbol{p}_n$ is true in a certain interpretation I_n having the set $\{0, 1, 2, \ldots\}$ of natural numbers as its domain.

3. $\text{ex}(\boldsymbol{p}_n)$ is true in every interpretation having $\{0, 1, 2, \ldots\}$ as domain.

4. $\boldsymbol{p}_n^*$ is valid, i.e., true in every interpretation whatever.

Here are the three steps.

Proof that condition 1 holds iff condition 2 does. In section 6-7 an interpretation was specified in which the premises of the inference associated with A_n are all true, and in which the conclusion of that inference is true or false depending on whether or not A_n eventually halts. That interpretation had $\{0, 1, 2, \ldots\}$ as its domain, assigned 0 as bearer to the name "o," assigned the successor function as value to the function symbol " ′ ," and assigned a set of $(r + 2)$tuples as extension to the predicate letter "R." At the end of Section 6-8 we modified this interpretation by dropping the function symbol " ′ " and adding in its stead the two-place predicate letter "S," to which the modified interpretation assigned as extension the set of all pairs of form n, $n + 1$, where n is in the domain. Call this interpetation "I_n." The premises of the "new-style" inference associated with A_n are all true in I_n, and its conclusion is true or false in I_n depending on whether or not A_n eventually halts. Now $\boldsymbol{p}_n$ is formed by replacing the second premise of the "new-style" inference by an equivalent statement as in instruction b, and conjoining that with the remaining premises together with further components whose conjunction is equivalent to the denial of the conclusion of the inference. Thus $\boldsymbol{p}_n$ is true in I_n iff A_n never halts.

Proof that condition 2 holds iff condition 3 does. The rules of valuation for existential generalizations (Sections 7-4 and 7-8) ensure that $\mathrm{ex}(\boldsymbol{p}_n)$ is true in I_n if $\boldsymbol{p}_n$ is. And since $\mathrm{ex}(\boldsymbol{p}_n)$ contains no symbols to which basic assignments of types 2 to 6 in Section 7-4 would be made, the truth value of $\mathrm{ex}(\boldsymbol{p}_n)$ in an interpretation will be entirely determined by basic assignment 1, i.e., the domain of that interpretation. Therefore $\mathrm{ex}(\boldsymbol{p}_n)$ will have the same truth value in *every* interpretation with domain $\{0, 1, 2, \ldots\}$ that it has in I_n.

Proof that condition 3 holds iff condition 4 does. As $\boldsymbol{p}_n^*$ is a conditional, it is true in all interpretations in which its antecedent, *den*, is false. Thus, $\boldsymbol{p}_n^*$ is true in all interpretations whose domains are not denumerable. Then $\boldsymbol{p}_n^*$ is valid iff it is true in all interpretations with denumerable domains. As its antecedent is true in all such interpretations, $\boldsymbol{p}_n^*$ will be valid iff its consequent, $\mathrm{ex}(\boldsymbol{p}_n)$, is true in all interpretations with denumerable domains. Then to prove conditions 3 and 4 equivalent, it suffices to observe (as in the remarks on enumerable infinity in Section 7-7) that truth in all interpretations with the particular denumerable domain $\{0, 1, 2, \ldots\}$ implies truth in all interpretations with denumerable domains of any sort.

Thus, $\boldsymbol{p}_n^*$ is valid iff A_n never halts. It follows that any sound, complete clerical routine for recognizing second-order validity of statements could be modified to yield what we saw to be impossible in Section 6-4, i.e., a sound, complete clerical routine for recognizing abacus programs that will never halt if started with all registers empty. We have proved Gödel's incompleteness theorem.*

---

* The proof uses an adaptation of a method suggested by Gisbert Hasenjaeger; see Hans Hermes, *Enumerability, Decidability, Computability*, Springer-Verlag, New York, 1965, sec. 26.

REFERENCES

Adams, Ernest: "The Logic of Conditionals," *Inquiry*, **8**:166–197, 1965.

——: "Subjunctive and Indicative Conditionals," *Foundations of Language*, **6**:89–94, 1970.

Boolos, George, and Richard Jeffrey: *Computability and Logic*, 2d ed., Cambridge University Press, Cambridge, 1980.

Church, Alonzo: "An Unsolvable Problem of Elementary Number Theory," *The American Journal of Mathematics*, **58**:345–363, 1936. (Reprinted in Davis, 1965.)

——: "A Note on the *Entscheidungsproblem*," *Journal of Symbolic Logic*, **1**:40–41, 1936; correction *ibid.*, 101–102. (Reprinted in Davis, 1965.)

Davidson, Donald, and Gilbert Harman (eds.): *The Logic of Grammar*, Dickenson, Encino, Calif., 1975.

Davis, Martin: *Computability and Unsolvability*, McGraw-Hill, New York, 1958.

—— (ed.): *The Undecidable*, Raven, Hewlett, N.Y., 1965.

Dreben, Burton, and Warren D. Goldfarb: *The Decision Problem*, Addison-Wesley, Reading, Mass., 1979.

Ellis, Brian: *Rational Belief Systems*, Basil Blackwell, Oxford, 1979.

Frege, Gottlob: *Begriffschrift*, Halle, 1879. (Translated in van Hijenoort, 1967.)

Geach, Peter T: *Reason and Argument*, University of California Press, Berkeley, 1976.

Gödel, Kurt: "Die Vollständigkeit der Axiome des logischen Funktionenkalküls," *Monatshefte für Mathematik und Physik*, **37**:349–360, 1930. (Translated in van Heijenoort, 1967.)

————: "Über formal unentscheidbare Sätze der Principia mathematica und verwandter System I," *Monatschefte für Mathematik und Physik*, **38**:173–198, 1931. (Translated in van Heijenoort, 1967.)

Grice, H. P.: William James Lectures, Harvard University, 1967 (unpublished).

————: "Logic and Conversation," in Davidson and Harman, pp. 64–75.

Hermes, Hans: *Enumerability, Decidability, Computability*, Springer-Verlag, Berlin, and Academic, New York, 1965.

Kleene, S. C.: "General Recursive Functions of Natural Numbers," *Mathematische Annalen*, **112**:727–742, 1936. (Reprinted with corrections and addenda in Davis, 1965.)

Kneale, William, and Martha Kneale: *The Development of Logic*, Clarendon, Oxford, 1962.

Lambek, Joachim: "How to Program an Infinite Abacus," *Canadian Mathematical Bulletin*, **4**:295–302, 1961.

Lewis, David K.: "Probabilities of Conditionals and Conditional Probabilities," *Philosophical Review*, **85**:297–315, 1976.

Lewis, Harry R.: *Unsolvable Classes of Quantificational Formulas*, Addison-Wesley, Reading, Mass., 1979.

Löwenheim, Leopold: "Über Möglichkeiten im Relativkalkül," *Mathematische Annalen*, **76**:447–470, 1915. (Translated in van Heijenoort, 1967.)

Markov, A. A.: "Theory of Algorithms (Russian)," *Tr. Mat. Inst. Steklov* **42** (1954). Translation: Office of Technical Services, U.S. Department of Commerce, Washington, D.C., 1962.

Melzak, Z. A.: "An Informal Arithmetical Approach to Computability and Computation," *Canadian Mathematical Bulletin*, **4**:279–294, 1961.

Mendelson, Elliott: *Introduction to Mathematical Logic*, 2d ed. Van Nostrand, Princeton, N.J., 1979.

Palmer, Jack, and Spencer Williams (words and music): "Everybody Loves My Baby," MCA Music, New York, 1924. For complete copyright information, see page *iv*.

Paul of Tarsus: Epistle to Titus.

Post, Emil: "Finite Combinatory Processes," *The Journal of Symbolic Logic*, **1**:103–105, 1936. (Reprinted in Davis, 1965.)

———: "Recursively Enumerable Sets of Positive Integers and Their Decision Problems," *Bulletin of the American Mathematical Society,* **50**:284–316, 1944. (Reprinted in Davis, 1965.)

Rado, Tibor: "On Non-computable Functions," *Bell System Technical Journal,* **41**:877–884, 1962.

Russell, Bertrand: "On Denoting," *Mind,* (N.S.) **14**:479–493, 1905.

———: "Mathematical Logic as Based on the Theory of Types," *American Journal of Mathematics,* **30**:222–262, 1908.

Smullyan, Raymond M.: *First-Order Logic,* Springer-Verlag, New York, 1968.

———: "What Is the Name of This Book?," Prentice-Hall, Englewood Cliffs, N.J., 1978.

Toledo, Sue: *Tableau Systems for First Order Number Theory and Certain Higher Order Theories,* Springer-Verlag, New York, 1975.

Trakhtenbrot, B. A.: *Algorithms and Automatic Computing Machines.* Heath, Boston, 1963.

Turing, Alan: "On Computable Numbers, with an Application to the Entscheidungsproblem," *Proceedings of the London Mathematical Society,* series 2, **42**:230–265, 1936: *ibid.,* **43**:544–546, 1937. (Reprinted in Davis, 1965.)

———: "Solvable and Unsolvable Problems," *Science News,* **31**:7–23, 1954.

van Heijenoort, Jan (ed.): *From Frege to Gödel: A Source Book of Mathematical Logic, 1897–1931,* Harvard University Press, Cambridge, Mass., 1967.

Whitehead, A. N., and Bertrand Russell: *Principia Mathematica,* vol. 1, Cambridge University Press, 1st ed., 1910; 2d ed., 1925.

INDEX

INDEX